WOKE
IS DEAD

WOKE
IS DEAD

How Common Sense Triumphed
in an Age of Total Madness

PIERS
MORGAN

HarperCollins*Publishers*

HarperCollins*Publishers*
1 London Bridge Street
London SE1 9GF

www.harpercollins.co.uk

HarperCollins*Publishers*
Macken House, 39/40 Mayor Street Upper
Dublin 1, D01 C9W8, Ireland

First published by HarperCollins*Publishers* 2025

25 2⬚ 27 28 29 LBC ⬚ 5 4 3 2

© Piers Morgan 2025

Piers Morgan asserts the moral right to
be identified as the author of this work

A catalogue record of this book is
available from the British Library

HB ISBN 978-0-00-855549-8
PB ISBN 978-0-00-855550-4

Printed and bound in the United States

For Miles,
The best of mates.

CONTENTS

PART THREE: UNCENSORED

PART FOUR: THE COMMON-SENSE REVOLUTION

Prologue

THE DON RISES

'Piers, we have a problem.'

6 NOVEMBER 2024

The cell phone rang out once, twice, three times ... nothing.

Four, five, six times ... nothing.

Seven, eight, nine times ... nothing.

Then, just as I was about to hang up, a hoarse and exhausted-sounding voice answered.

'Piers!' croaked president-elect Donald Trump.

We'd shared hundreds of phone calls in the past 20 years. But the one we had the morning after his comeback win wasn't any normal call.

This was an extraordinary moment in history, not just for Trump, but for America and the world. He had just become only the second president after Grover Cleveland (132 years ago!) to secure a non-consecutive second term in office.

1

'This is quite something, right?' he chuckled.

'Yes, it is,' I chuckled back. 'I've been watching TV all morning and can barely believe what I'm seeing. I just wanted to personally congratulate you on pulling off the greatest comeback in political history. You're now officially the Tiger Woods of politics.'

'Thank you!' he laughed. 'I appreciate that very much, especially coming from you because I know you always say what you really think.'

I reminded him that it had been 17 years since we'd met on *Celebrity Apprentice*.

'It's been one hell of a journey since then,' I said.

'Yes, it has,' he replied, 'for both of us!'

'Well, a bit more for you than me!' I said.

Certainly, if someone had said back in 2008 that Donald J. Trump, a TV star and realtor with no political experience, would win the 2016 election against the most-qualified candidate in history, Hillary Clinton, then lose the 2020 election after a once-in-a-century pandemic, then refuse to accept the result, and help fuel – wittingly or unwittingly – a deadly 'Stop the Steal!' riot at the US Capitol, then mount the most extraordinary comeback campaign as his enemies first tried to jail him – making him the first former US president in history to be convicted of a federal crime over hush money payments to a porn star – and then tried to assassinate him in two attempts within a few weeks, only for him to win a crushing victory at the polls in November 2024 ... well, I suspect we'd have all thought that person was bonkers.

Yet, incredibly, that is exactly what happened.

'How do you feel?' I asked.

Trump's not big on 'feelings', but I was genuinely curious what this all meant to him on a personal level. Nobody in history has ever been given a second chance at life and the US presidency in just four months.

He paused and then repeated the question.

'How do I feel? Nobody has asked me that ... you know, I feel great!'

'I loved what you said about common sense,' I said. 'I think that really hit home with voters.'

'Well, it's true,' Trump replied.

And he was right. It is.

Trump's implausible comeback is probably the single most vivid illustration of woke's demise. It slammed the door shut on a frenzied decade of outrage, sensitivity and censorship with a defiant barrage of straight-talking common-sense ideas that many people feared were gone for good.

You don't have to like Trump or his politics to step back and appreciate the symbolic significance. How could *he* of all people return triumphantly to the highest office in the world in the era of MeToo, Black Lives Matter, 'My Truth' and endlessly offended cancel culture? The answer is: because that era is over. Ha!

11 APRIL 2022

I was standing inside the gilded, gold-plated confines of President Donald Trump's exclusive Mar-a-Lago private member's resort in Palm Beach, Florida, and one of my production team was brandishing a document with a concerned look on his face.

'What's that?' I asked, bemused.

'This is a collection of quotes you've apparently said about President Trump in the past two years. Someone sent it to him in the last hour, and the quotes are not good. In fact, they're really bad.'

I was due to start an interview with Trump in precisely eight minutes, and it was intended to be a blockbuster exclusive to rocket-launch my new global TV show, *Piers Morgan Uncensored* on 25 April 2022. But as I hurriedly scanned the three-page white paper document, my heart sank.

There were several dozen comments from me, taken from columns I'd written and interviews I'd given, in which I was savagely critical of Trump's conduct in the last year of his presidency, from his woeful handling of the coronavirus pandemic to his refusal to accept defeat in the 2020 election, and the appalling 6 January riot at the US Capitol which followed.

'Is he going to cancel the interview?' I asked, trying not to fret.

'I don't know,' came the reply. 'But he is VERY upset.'

'See if I can go and talk to him about it,' I suggested.

Twenty minutes later, I was sitting in Trump's office.

Normally, he'd greet me with a cheery smile and the words 'How's my Champ?' because I was his first victorious Celebrity Apprentice on the series that made him a TV superstar.

But this time, there were no such welcoming pleasantries.

He was staring at me across his desk with undisguised fury, clutching the document entitled 'Piers Morgan Comments About President Trump'.

'What the fuck IS this?' he snarled.

Then he began slowly reading out some of the quotes.

'Trump's a supreme narcissist ...'

Pause.

'His pathetic antics in the past few weeks since losing the election in November have been utterly contemptible.'

Pause.

'Trump's now too dangerous; he's morphed into a monster that I no longer recognise as someone I considered to be a friend and thought I knew.'

Pause.

'He's now acting like a mafia mob boss.'

Pause.

'And all because Donald's stupendous ego couldn't accept losing and sent him nuts.'

Each time he paused, he peered over the document at me, with mounting rage in his eyes.

When I won Trump's inaugural *Celebrity Apprentice* show in 2008, his final words to me as he announced the result were: 'Piers, you're a vicious guy. I've seen it. You're tough. You're smart. You're probably brilliant. I'm not sure. You're certainly not diplomatic. But you did an amazing job. And you beat the hell out of everybody ... you're the Celebrity Apprentice.'

When he won the 2016 election, I returned the favour by sending him a card saying: 'Well, Donald, you're a vicious guy. I've seen it. You're tough. You're smart. You're probably brilliant. I'm not sure. You're certainly not diplomatic. But you did an amazing job. And you beat the hell out of everybody ... you're the President of the United States.'

So, we had a reasonable understanding of each other's personalities, good and bad.

And it wasn't like we'd never had a spat.

He unfollowed me on Twitter (he only followed around 50 accounts at the time, and I was the only Brit, so this didn't go unnoticed!) in April 2020 after he'd proposed using household disinfectant to fight Covid, and I'd hammered him in a column for spreading 'batshit crazy coronavirus cure theories that will get people killed.'

But a few months later, right before the 2020 election, he called me for a lengthy chat and chuckled about how 'mean and nasty' I'd been about him, so I mistakenly assumed he didn't really mind me verbally whacking him from time to time.

Wrong!

I'd never seen him so livid or felt so uncomfortable in his presence as I did right now in his office.

He was almost foaming at the mouth and kept shaking his head slowly and menacingly at me.

There was no point in trying to deny the quotes. I'd said them, and I'd meant them.

'I've always been critical of you when I've felt you deserved it,' I eventually said, 'but as you know, I've also written and said many supportive things about you too. This is a one-sided hatchet job designed to stop you doing our interview.'

'It's definitely a hatchet job,' he retorted, 'on ME!'

Then he read another line: 'January 7, 2021 – President Trump needs to be removed from office. As soon as possible ... through new emergency articles of impeachment, which would have the additional benefit of barring him from ever running for the presidency again.'

'REMOVED FROM OFFICE?!' he shouted. 'BARRED FROM EVER RUNNING FOR PRESIDENT AGAIN?!'

Then he threw down the document and threw me a look of withering contempt.

'I thought we were friends?' he shouted. 'This is so disloyal! After all I've done for you? Why would you say all this about me?'

'I thought what you did was wrong,' I replied, feeling myself beginning to sweat.

This wasn't going well.

It looked for sure like Trump was about to cancel the interview, which would have been a massive waste of time and money for me and our team – leaving me an even more massive hole for my first show.

I was desperately thinking of some way to salvage things.

'I don't intend our interview to be confrontational,' I said. 'A lot of time has passed since I said those things, and a lot has happened in the meantime.'

'Why should I do it at all?' he scoffed. 'You're not real. You're a fake.'

'No, I'm just brutally honest.'

'DIS-honest!'

We stared at each other for a few seconds, his eyes boring into mine with all the warmth of an Arctic glacier.

It was time to change the mood music.

'There are a lot of positive things I want to discuss with you too,' I stammered.

'Like WHAT?' he snapped back.

'Like your recent golf hole-in-one. Your playing partner, Ernie Els, was raving about it.'

Trump sat bolt upright.

'He was? Where?'

'In a local newspaper interview I read this morning. He said it was a brilliant shot, and you played really well ...'

'I did, I did.'

'Was that your first hole-in-one?'

'No! I've had seven!'

Seven?!

'Amazing,' I replied. 'Congrats! Ernie said you were the best presidential golfer he had played with ...'

Trump instantly ordered one of his aides to get him some copies of the newspaper containing the interview.

Then he clapped his hands.

'OK, I guess I'll still do the interview. I don't know why, honestly, but I'll see you down there.'

Thank you, Ernie! I felt a huge wave of relief as I headed back to my team.

Ten minutes later, President Trump arrived in the interview room and acted like nothing had happened as we posed for smiling photos together. But I could sense he was still very wound up, and there was none of the usual bonhomie between us that I was used to in our many previous encounters.

I'd been promised 20 minutes and feared he would cut that down to punish me. But in the end, I got 75 minutes, by far the longest time I'd ever had with him on camera, and it was a fascinating, often riveting, and sometimes hilarious series of exchanges with arguably the world's most famous person as we talked about everything from Ukraine, Putin, Kim Jong-un and nuclear weapons, to the Royals, transgender athletes, Twitter and Joe Biden.

For the first hour or so, it was a perfectly normal interview. Trump displayed all the forthright style and brash humour that first propelled him into the White House and certainly showed no sign of losing any of his fabled energy.

I also agreed with him about many issues, as I have done in the past.

But the interview took a dramatic downward turn when I finally brought up his refusal to accept defeat in 2020 and the appalling scenes on 6 January.

I told him I believed he lost the supposedly 'rigged, stolen' election, I repeatedly pointed out his failure to produce any evidence of the widespread voter fraud he insists occurred to rob him of his presidency, and I blamed his refusal to admit defeat for the deadly riots at the Capitol.

'Then you're a FOOL!' he sneered. 'And you haven't studied!'

He was back to the furious Trump he'd been in his office and branded me a fool six more times, in between calling Senate minority leader Mitch McConnell 'stupid', and his former vice-president Mike Pence 'foolish and weak'.

Now abandoning any pretence at cordiality, Trump ranted that he was far more honest than me and again sneered that I wasn't 'real', before haranguing me for exceeding our 20 minutes.

He tried to end things by jumping to his feet, removing his microphone, and declaring 'That's it!' before I reminded him that we hadn't discussed his hole-in-one, so he then sat down again and chatted very happily about his golfing glory for a few minutes, before abruptly jumping to his feet again, and barking at the shocked crew: 'TURN THE CAMERAS OFF!'

Then he turned on his heels, and sloped angrily off through a side door, loudly muttering 'SO dishonest ...' Apparently, he was later heard denouncing me as a 'scumbag' and saying he wished he'd never done the interview.

But I thought it was the best one we've ever done together; all the tension created by the damning document gave it a crackle and energy that made for compelling television.

As for who sent him the document in the first place, Trump told me it came from 'a friend in London' and gave it to me to 'keep as a souvenir of your treachery'.

Mysteriously, it contains two random, very positive comparative quotes from British politician Nigel Farage who was by then working as a presenter for UK news network GB News.

Oh, and by an extraordinary coincidence, Farage happened to have dinner with Trump at Mar-a-Lago on 8 April, just three days before I was there.

You don't need to be a rigged election conspiracy theorist to work out who went home, compiled the damning dossier, and sent it to him.

Farage later admitted he'd done it and had told him not to do the interview. This seemed especially treacherous given that when Farage himself had interviewed Trump a few months earlier, I sent him a text saying: 'Great hit with The Don, congrats,' to which he replied: 'Thanks, that's very good of you.'

The next day, I sent Trump an email thanking him for his time and included these words: 'You had every right to get annoyed and call me a fool for not believing the election was stolen from you, but I also have every right to my opinion, and I wasn't going to lie to your face just to avoid annoying you. The best friends are the most honest/critical ones, not the sycophants.'

He didn't reply.

But once the interview aired, garnering huge global attention thanks to me heavily promoting our fiery exchanges, he piled into me with a series of increasingly savage attacks, culminating in a rally speech in Nebraska where he raged: 'This crazy Piers Morgan, did you see that show? He's sort of had it. I think Piers is over the hill. I did him a favour. I didn't want to do his stupid show. He opened with great ratings when he did me and then after my interview was finished he bombed and he's now down over 70 per cent. And maybe they'll someday learn that …

Maybe they should hire me as an anchor ... We'd get the greatest ratings.'

And he's right: *Donald Trump Uncensored* would be TV gold.

Our relationship now feels very far from golden. Perhaps we'll never speak again?

I hope not. Donald Trump remains one of the world's most interesting people, and I still wouldn't bet against him somehow returning to the White House in the greatest comeback since Lazarus.

PART ONE
THE WOKE TIMEBOMB

Whenever I think of a perfect way to describe woke, my mind returns to a conversation I had on a west London street, shortly after I left *Good Morning Britain* for expressing my opinion that Meghan Markle may not be the most comfortable bedfellow with the truth – be that her truth, my truth, or anyone else's truth.

An elderly but very elegant and sprightly Australian lady bounded up to me and declared: 'The problem with all these wokies is they just want to suck all the joy out of life. Don't let them get away with it, Mr Morgan!'

I gave her my word that I wouldn't, and I think I've kept my word ever since.

Chapter 1

PEAK WOKE

*'I don't want anybody here to watch this and think
we're attacking you for being racist.'*

When I was forced out of *Good Morning Britain* after
refusing to apologise for disbelieving Princess Pinocchio
Meghan Markle, and a record 57,000 people complained
about me to the TV regulator Ofcom, a friend forwarded
me an email from Britain's top criminal lawyer, John
Kelsey-Fry KC, which read:

'If you happen to be speaking to Piers Morgan anytime
soon, would you be good enough to make clear to him
that 57,000 brainwashed complainants do not represent
right-thinking people in this country.

'As it happens, I agree wholeheartedly with everything
Piers said on this particular topic, but that is not the point.

'The views Piers expressed were legitimate and reasonable by reference to what was and was not in the Winfrey
interview. The idea that one is forbidden from holding and
expressing those views simply because to do so involves

doubting, however sincerely, allegations of racism or claims of mental illness is simply contemptible.

'The inevitable consequence of such a prohibition is that so long as one complains of racism or mental illness one's word must be accepted without question.

'This is unspeakable – as, it seems, are all contrary views.

'The wickedness of all this was exposed by the attacks on Piers. Everyone is entitled to their own assessment of the accuracy and reliability of the Meghan Markle complaints (in so far as there was sufficient specificity to judge). However, Piers has not been allowed the same entitlement – his contrary view was asserted to be driven by a personal animus against MM, i.e. not genuine, false, confected for revenge.

'This is iniquitous and demonstrates a serious disease which has infected public debate – "I am right, what is more I am so right nobody can genuinely disagree with me, ergo if anybody expresses a contrary view it is false and driven by racism, animus or some other malign motive."

'The result is that people are frightened to speak their minds for fear of being labelled racist, uncaring or malign.

'If people like Piers are driven out of public debate there will be no debate. There will be no probing, no questioning, no proper analysis – only the self-appointed thought police who have commandeered the airways and the cowed, literally silent majority.

'I never thought to hear myself say this but we need the Piers Morgans of this world more than ever.'

All flattery aside, it was a forensic prosecution of woke's corrosive impact on free speech and an eloquent explanation of the disastrous mess it dragged us into. My now-infamous walkout came at the peak of the madness.

Women were to be taken unquestioningly at their word about any claim. Gender, mental health and racial status were impenetrable force fields. Self-identifying as a pansexual moon donkey entitled you not only to a fair hearing but the equivalent of a standing ovation on Twitter. Anybody who questioned the consensus was to be hunted down and flogged by the permanently offended.

In America, my long-time friend Sharon Osbourne was fired from her show *The Talk* on CBS, after she reacted angrily to her black co-host Sheryl Underwood accusing her of supporting a racist – me!

'I don't know what he's uttered that's racist,' Sharon said. 'Tell me what he said that's racist?'

'It is not the exact words of racism,' replied Underwood, 'it's the implication and reaction to it.'

'I don't understand,' said a bemused Sharon. 'If Piers doesn't like someone, and they happen to be black, does that make him a racist?'

'No,' said Underwood.

'Right, so why can't it be that he just doesn't like her? Why does it have to be racist?'

There was no answer to this question. Instead, in a moment of stupendous disingenuousness, Underwood said: 'I don't want anybody here to watch this and think we're attacking you for being racist.'

Sharon chuckled ruefully. 'I think it's too late, that seed's already sown.'

Yes, it was, and it was sown very deliberately, just as it had been about me.

Sharon was disgracefully bullied into making a grovelling apology, but all that did was fuel her woke tormentors into an even more ravenous bloodlust that required her to hire extra security after being bombarded with death threats.

Two weeks later, she was fired.

The conservative commentator Ben Shapiro texted me: 'How dare you criticise Meghan Markle for tearing apart the British crown for her own personal gain based on literally zero evidence other than her word? I mean, we know how honest and altruistic and non-self-serving she has been for the past few years, so her word is basically gold where I am concerned. And we also know that to deny allegations of racism is in and of itself racism, which is not at all Orwellian. We must never, EVER question anyone's sense of personal self-invention, the world must conform to individual self-creation, rather than individuals conforming to factual reality.'

Never let it be said that Americans don't do sarcasm.

The issue of gender has been weaponised just as maliciously as racism to silence criticism. It's what caused Harry Potter author J. K. Rowling to be subjected to horrendous abuse and threats after standing up for women's rights.

And it's what led to US swimmer Riley Gaines, an equally brave and vocal opponent of trans athletes competing as women, feeling 'violated' by sharing a locker room with a 'fully naked' trans swimmer and even having to be escorted by police to a classroom, where she sheltered for three hours from a threatening crowd of howling protestors before she was able to safely leave a speaking venue.

The whole ideology was imposed with voracious hunger by the big institutions that govern us, as evidenced by the medical profession and its sinister creeping linguistic assault on women.

Mothers were renamed 'birthing people', breastfeeding became 'chestfeeding', and medical bible *The Lancet* even had a cover about 'bodies with vaginas'.

In Britain, our much-vaunted National Health Service (NHS) dropped the word 'women' from its main online health advice for women being treated for cervical, womb and ovarian cancers – despite the fact that ONLY women born to female bodies suffer from these diseases, because only women have cervixes, wombs and ovaries.

This was supposedly done to avoid causing offence to transgender or non-binary people who don't wish to be called women.

But what about the offence this might cause actual biological women with breasts and vaginas (spoiler alert: that's ALL women) who DO want to be called women?

Where were THEIR rights in all this?

The Johns Hopkins University in Baltimore, reputed to be one of the world's best medical and scientific hubs of academic excellence, decided to unilaterally redefine the word 'lesbian' to be 'more inclusive'.

In its official online glossary of LGBTQ+ terminology, it said a lesbian was 'a non-man attracted to non-men'. It explained: 'While past definitions refer to "lesbian" as a woman who is emotionally, romantically, and/or sexually attracted to other women, this updated definition includes non-binary people who may also identify with this label.'

Obviously, this egregious load of virtue-signalling woke piffle was bad enough.

But it got worse.

How did the same LGBTQ+ glossary define a gay man? It said: 'A man who is emotionally, romantically, sexually, affectionately, or relationally attracted to other men, or who identifies as a member of the gay community.'

So, let me get this straight (pun intended ...).

If you're a lesbian, you're a non-man.

If you're a gay man, you're a man.

But what nobody's allowed to be ... is a woman.

And this misogynistic garbage was coming from one of the planet's supposedly smartest medical brains? People who literally study biology every day of their lives?

Dr Irwin Redlener, president emeritus of the Children's Health Fund, told the *New York Times* that these sorts of linguistic interventions reflect 'liberals going overboard to create definitions and divisions'.

He added: 'It actually exacerbates divisions rather than accomplishing something useful.'

Exactly.

And if you don't fully grasp the problem, here's a simple test: go up to Megan Rapinoe, Martina Navratilova, or Cynthia Nixon, call them a 'non-man', and see what happens ...

Another of the many absurd aspects to wokeism is the belief in limitless self-identity: the notion that anyone can identify as whatever they like, regardless of science or biology, and must be respected.

Of course, this only applied to woke causes.

In the UK, there was an outbreak of 'furry fandom', a craze that involved kids at school identifying as animals. An audio recording emerged of a conversation between students and a woke teacher at Rye College in southern England after one of the kids refused to accept a classmate's claim that she was a cat.

'How dare you?!' snapped the teacher. 'You've just really upset someone by questioning their identity.'

The young student replied: 'If they want to identify as a cat then they are genuinely unwell – crazy.'

'Gender is not linked to the parts that you were born with,' the teacher raged, 'gender is how you identify.'

The student disagreed, saying: 'If you have a vagina, you're a girl, and if you have a penis, you're a boy.'

To which the enraged teacher snapped back: 'You are talking about the fact that cisgender is the norm, that you identify with the sexual organ you were born with ... which is really despicable.'

He then warned: 'You need to have a proper educational conversation about equality, diversity, and inclusion because I'm not having that expressed in my lesson. If you don't like it, you need to go to a different school.'

Ironically, as I read this, I began to hiss and bare my feline fangs in fury.

What in God's name was going on at our schools?

Why the hell were these teachers tolerating this deluded nonsense?

Where are the parents of these kids who've adopted such brain-warped thinking?

The next time a child identifies as a cat at school, they should be told that as a mark of respect for their new identity, they will be taken out of the classroom and put in a large cage with other actual cats who want to scratch and bite them all day long, they'll be given water and tuna chunks for lunch, and must use a litter tray for a toilet.

Trust me, they'll be re-identifying as humans again by teatime.

That teacher was emblematic of one of wokeism's biggest flaws: it denies reality and promotes fantasy. And never has this been more insidious than in the systematic erosion of women's rights at the altar of trans-genderism.

In the UK, a supposed 'transgender woman' named Isla Bryson was jailed for raping two women.

In fact, he was a male rapist named Adam Graham who suddenly decided to self-identify as female at his trial to successfully get himself put in a Scottish women's prison among future potential female targets, like a fox being locked up in a hen coop.

Graham was moved back to a male prison after an intense media furore, but not before Scotland's First Minister Nicola Sturgeon had at first refused to say he was a man, then made a humiliating U-turn. She would eventually resign for several reasons.

How could a trailblazing female politician, who'd fought for women's rights her whole life, have failed women so badly?

The answer is simple: she was too terrified of the woke brigade.

But the perils of this moral cowardice are obvious.

In the US, a serial killer named Harvey Marcelin killed and decapitated a woman in Brooklyn. He'd earlier been accused of the attempted rape of an eight-year-old girl, and then raping and killing a girlfriend.

On his release from prison, he killed a homeless sex worker and was jailed again. But he was released, again, 33 years later, and because he now identified as a transgender woman, he was shockingly placed in a women's homeless shelter.

And then, predictably, he killed again.

In his trial, Marcelin was described as an '83-year-old woman' and so the case was reported as an 83-year-old woman gruesomely murdering another woman.

It wasn't.

It was a man pretending to be a woman who murdered a woman.

Then there's the scandal of 'gender dysphoria' clinics, which became so alarmingly prevalent across America and Europe, with thousands of children being irreversibly drugged and mutilated each year because barbaric doctors fuelled, and commercialised, their supposed transgender 'leanings'.

In London, the notorious Tavistock Gender and Identity Development Service was forced to close after a report concluded that 97 per cent of ALL the young patients there suffered from myriad other conditions like autism and depression.

It was an utter disgrace, aided and abetted by the attempts to change how we think and speak. Anybody insisting you use phrases like 'birthing parent' is forcing you to implicitly agree with it. And these subtle impositions to rewire our brains were everywhere, as was the pile of reputations and careers thrown onto the cancel culture bonfire.

Chapter 2

HOW WOKEISM HELPED ELECT A PRESIDENT

'You know, we're the party of common sense.'

All of which brings me back to the morning of 6 November 2024.

I'd gone to bed in a New York hotel room after Trump's 2 a.m. victory speech and been up again since 6 a.m. watching the TV coverage simultaneously across multiple networks on various devices. And one thing became ever clearer as the morning wore on: Trump hadn't just won, he'd flatlined his Democratic opponent Kamala Harris into complete and utter humiliating defeat.

The Republicans had obviously prevailed in the key electoral college vote, and thus regained the White House. But it also looked likely, as was later confirmed, that they were going to win back control of the Senate, retain their majority in the House of Representatives, and even triumph in the popular vote, which had eluded Republicans since 2004. And they did it by increasing support from groups right across the political demographic, especially Latinos, African Americans and younger men.

It wasn't just a stunning validation for Trump, still smarting from the 2020 election loss that he refused to accept, it was also a stunning repudiation of Harris, and her left-wing progressive agenda that Trump's most vocal and influential campaign backer, Elon Musk, dubbed the 'woke mind virus'.

And something Trump said in his victory speech really resonated with me.

Explaining why he thought he'd won so convincingly with so many different groups, he said: 'It was a historic realignment, uniting citizens of all backgrounds around a common core of common sense. You know, we're the party of common sense.'

BINGO!

The two biggest issues in this US election were the economy, and the way ruinously high inflation during Joe Biden's term had sparked a cost-of-living crisis that ravaged the wallets of millions of Americans; and immigration, for which Biden had presided over an undeniable disaster on the southern border that contributed to an estimated ten million people in total entering the US illegally.

But there was a third issue which I had felt for a long time could be hugely impactful too, and it was that many Americans had grown sick and tired of insidious woke bullshit.

Trump's victory laid bare a cold, irrefutable reality: wokeism is the very opposite of common sense.

What IS common sense?

Derived from the Latin words *sensus communis*, dictionaries define the phrase as 'knowledge, judgement, and taste which is more or less universal, that is independent of specialized knowledge, training, or the like; normal native intelligence; which is held more or less without reflection or argument'.

In other words, simple stuff that makes us think: 'Yes, that makes sense.'

In a world where the scourge of wokeism rendered so many people weak-willed, work-shy, lacking in the resilience, resolve and perseverance required to navigate life's travails, and totally devoid of basic common sense, Trump has all of those qualities in abundance.

Whatever people think of him, and there is rarely a middle 'I'm not really sure' ground with Trump, nobody can credibly doubt his strength of character, ferocious work ethic, or astonishing ability to barrel through and bounce back from adversity.

And his 'core of common sense' has undeniable mass appeal, even if the way he articulates it can be overly, and unnecessarily, inflammatory.

Trump trusts his gut instinct, even when his closest aides are screaming at him to change course, and that, above all else, is why he wins.

We've been friends for nearly two decades now, albeit with a few 'relationship wobbles' along the way. The last wobble, and our biggest, over the fiery 2022 Mar-a-Lago interview, ended when he replied, an entire month late, to my email requesting another interview after Queen Elizabeth II died in September that year, with a handwritten note back saying simply: 'Piers, she was great, best wishes Donald.'

But a few months later, he called me out of the blue for a long chat that began with the words: 'Hi Piers, it's your favourite president, are we good?'

And we were.

I've always understood why some people can't stomach Trump, but I don't understand the venomous hysteria of his wokest opponents. They brand Trump a fascist, but ironically, they themselves became the fascists – shaming and cancelling anyone and anything that dares to deviate from or defy their narrow, blinkered, heavily censored and joyless worldview.

They call themselves liberals, but their behaviour is so antithetical to liberal values it's beyond parody.

They demand diversity, equity and inclusion but rush to exclude anyone they don't like and play the race card at every opportunity. Diversity, Equity and Inclusion has become a template for encouraging mediocrity over meritocracy, and nobody better personifies this than Kamala Harris, who Joe Biden made no secret of choosing as his vice-president because of her gender and skin colour, not because she was the best candidate for the job.

In the woke world, losers are winners, weakness is a virtue, and strength is a shameful thing to be despised and rejected. Long-suffering Americans who've endured this rancid twaddle for years finally rose up and said, ENOUGH!

They turned to Trump in such huge numbers, and from right across the age, race and gender divide, because they understood that for all his faults, at his core – as he said in his victory speech – there does indeed lie an instinctive common-sense set of beliefs they agree with.

A country needs secure borders, wars are ruinous, taxes are too high, governments are bloated, criminals should be caught and punished, meritocracy beats mediocrity, and a nuclear family is better than a broken home.

I knew for sure that Trump was going to win when I attended my first ever political rally, his huge star-studded event at Madison Square Garden in the middle of New York City, nine days before polling. I'd just arrived in the US for my show's election coverage and I wanted to see how Trump was welcomed in a Democrat city packed with his fiercest critics.

In 2016, hundreds of thousands of protestors had marched in New York to register their rage at Trump's victory over Hillary Clinton. I expected similar scenes at the MSG given that liberals had spent a year branding Trump the new Hitler and his supporters a bunch of Nazis and fascists.

I mean, if you genuinely think someone is the new Hitler, and Hitler may be about to get re-elected as your President, then you'd probably hit the streets to protest, right? Especially as Hillary had declared it would be a Nazi-loving, Jew-abusing hate-fest.

'One other thing that you'll see next week,' she told CNN, 'is Trump actually re-enacting the Madison Square Garden rally in 1939.'

She was referring to the infamous night at the MSG some months before World War II broke out when a group called the German-American Bund held a rally supposedly to celebrate George Washington's 207th birthday, but which in fact was a grotesquely antisemitic celebration of the ascent of Hitler's Third Reich Nazi government.

It was a despicable comparison for Clinton to make, but entirely in keeping with liberals' incessant and hysterical demonisation of Trump as a dangerous existential threat to American democracy.

But despite her attempt to whip liberals into a Nazi-fearing frenzy, nothing happened.

The streets were full alright, but with jubilant Trump supporters.

'I don't see no stinking Nazis in here!' bellowed the late wrestling legend Hulk Hogan on stage.

I didn't see any stinking Nazis either.

Instead I actually saw a lot of Jewish people and a fair few pro-Israel banners, which would have looked a little out of place had it been a Nazi rally.

That didn't stop MSNBC shamefully juxtaposing Trump rally footage with the 1939 footage. 'That jamboree happening right now,' said one of their anchors, 'is particularly chilling because in 1939, more than 20,000 supporters of a different fascist leader, Adolf Hitler, packed the Garden for a so-called pro-America rally.'

Trump has been an outspoken supporter of Israel, his son-in-law Jared Kushner is Jewish, and his daughter Ivanka converted to Judaism when she married him. There was even an actual Holocaust survivor, Jerry Wartski, in the crowd.

What kind of warped mind thinks it's OK to tell a man like him he's at a Nazi rally?

The last time I was at Madison Square Garden was the day after Trump's 2016 win. I was at a New York Knicks basketball game and found myself sitting next to comedian Chris Rock, so I asked him why he thought Trump had won.

'If someone's murdered eight people,' he said, 'don't go around saying he's murdered nine.'

Obviously, he didn't mean Trump had actually murdered anyone. He just meant there is plenty to legitimately criticise him about without absurdly exaggerating his danger.

But the truth is that liberals don't seem to know any other way.

A secret service agent told me that just 150 protestors turned up at the MSG to register their dismay at the new Hitler. Trump had crushed his critics into supine submission and I now felt certain he was about to win big.

And the other thing I knew for certain was that the woke brigade would once again throw their collective toys out of the stroller the moment he did. I was right about that too.

Chapter 3

BRAVE NEW WORLD

'We've finally worked out that women are actually women, so please do fuck off.'

It started with the howling.

Video after video of hysterical, mainly female Kamala Harris voters literally shrieking dementedly into their phone cameras and posting their tormented anguish to the world.

Then they started shaving their hair off, borrowing from the radical feminist 4B Movement originating in South Korea.

Then they vowed never to have sex with Trump supporters again.

'Fuck being skinny,' shouted one in a viral TikTok clip, 'fuck being hot, fuck being all the things that the patriarchy wants us to be, 'cause clearly they don't give a shit about us. Stop dating men, stop having sex with men, stop talking to men, divorce your husbands, leave your fucking boyfriends, leave them!'

I hesitate to point out the bleeding obvious here: that no man in their right mind would want to be around such an unhinged lunatic anyway.

Then came the liberal exodus from Elon Musk's X – led by author Stephen King, who declared: 'I'm leaving Twitter. Tried to stay, but the atmosphere has just become too toxic.'

At which point, I heard another piercing howl, as irony died.

The same Mr King has, in my opinion, been one of the foremost contributors to that toxic atmosphere for years, spewing what I consider to be aggressively worded bile at anyone who disagrees with his self-righteous worldview.

In the UK, the boycott was even more amusing as the left-wing *Guardian* newspaper quit X after offering therapy counselling to staff traumatised by Trump's win.

If all this sounds completely mad, it's because it is.

And it's been fuelled by a liberal-skewed media that also lost its mind.

'The source of this [hysteria and delusion] has been mainstream media,' Dr Drew Pinsky told Fox News host Sean Hannity. 'The American public has been propagandized to the point that they literally have become mentally ill. And the thing about delusionality is it can't be reasoned with. We have literally been through a stage of delusion that started with the first Trump presidency. It was put into absolute orbit with Covid.'

He's right.

These people have had their brains fried by eight years of three very damaging medical conditions: Trump

Derangement Syndrome, and two viruses – Coronavirus and the Woke Mind Virus.

And it's sent them utterly stark-raving bonkers.

The week after the election, in a nadir for even TDS sufferers, MSNBC presenter Joy Reid (who later got fired, I assume to put herself out of her own perpetual Trump-detesting misery) interviewed a Yale University psychiatrist who solemnly advised viewers to snub family members who voted for Trump over the upcoming Thanksgiving holidays.

'There is a societal norm that if somebody is your family that they are entitled to your time and I think the answer is absolutely not,' said Dr Amanda Calhoun. 'So, if you are going into a situation where you have family members, where you have close friends who you know have voted in ways that are against you … it's completely fine to not be around those people.'

As Reid nodded along enthusiastically to this crazed shrink's outlandish claptrap, I realised neither of them could help themselves, the woke madness was in too deep.

Nothing illustrated this more comically than when five of the six distraught hosts of ABC's *The View* trotted out in funereal black clothing the day after Trump won, because they were in mourning.

How did they not understand how ridiculous this looked given that the election result proved the majority of Americans didn't agree with them?

I don't pretend that Trump is everyone's cup of tea. He has a bombastic, confrontational rhetorical style that can be aggressive, rude and sometimes downright offensive.

And he has a unique ability to send his haters into violent spasms of uncontrolled rage, which he relishes.

Hollywood star Dennis Quaid summed it up well when he told me in an *Uncensored* interview: 'People might call him an asshole – but he's my asshole.'

Trump's win led to instant surrender from many who had enthusiastically enforced the woke ideology. One of the most notable examples was META boss Mark Zuckerberg, who had banned Trump from all the company's social media platforms – including Facebook and Instagram – after the 6 January riots.

First, Zuckerberg went to Mar-a-Lago to kiss the Trump ring over dinner.

The next month, he donated $1 million to Trump's inauguration fund.

Then, right before the inauguration, which Zuckerberg attended, he issued a very personal statement, sensationally admitting that the so-called 'independent' fact-checkers he'd hired to check facts on his platforms, were themselves so partisan against Trump, he was going to fire them and replace them with the same community notes system for fact-checking that Elon Musk created when he bought Twitter.

'After Trump first got elected in 2016, the legacy media wrote nonstop about how misinformation was a threat to democracy,' Zuckerberg said. 'We tried in good faith to address those concerns without becoming the arbiters of truth, but the fact-checkers have just been too politically biased and have destroyed more trust than they've created, especially in the US.'

This was truly staggering!

Zuckerberg was confessing that the very people he'd brought in to stop disinformation being spread by Donald Trump and his supporters were themselves disseminating disinformation.

Ironically, they were twisting facts against the supposed fact-twisters to suit their own woke agendas.

Zuckerberg added: 'We're going to work with President Trump to push back on governments around the world. They're going after American companies and pushing to censor more. The US has the strongest constitutional protections for free expression in the world. Europe has an ever-increasing number of laws, institutionalizing censorship, and making it difficult to build anything innovative there. Latin American countries have secret courts that can order companies to quietly take things down. China has censored our apps from even working in the country. The only way that we can push back on this global trend is with the support of the US government, and that's why it's been so difficult over the past four years when even the US government has pushed for censorship. By going after us and other American companies, it has emboldened other governments to go even further. But now, we have the opportunity to restore free expression, and I'm excited to take it.'

The irony of this last entreaty almost made my head explode. This was the same Zuckerberg who had censored Trump and his supporters in the first place, and so emphatically prohibited their freedom of expression.

The weirdest thing about wokeism is that those who slavishly espouse it don't seem to realise how fatal it is to achieving political success.

Former British Prime Minister Tony Blair wrote a very good piece for the *New Statesman* about this in which he argued: 'A progressive party seeking power which looks askance at the likes of Trevor Phillips, Sara Khan or JK Rowling is not going to win. Progressive politics needs to debate these cultural questions urgently and openly. It needs to push back strongly against those who will try to shout down the debate.

Earlier in the article he'd said: 'There is a big culture battle going on. Progressive folk tend to wince at terms such as "woke" and "political correctness", but the normal public knows exactly what they mean. And the battle is being fought on ground defined by the right because sensible progressives don't want to be on the field at all.

'The consequence of this is that the "radical" progressives, who are quite happy to fight on that ground, carry the progressive standard. The fact that it ensures continued right-wing victory doesn't deter them at all. On the contrary, it gives them a heightened sense of righteousness, like political kamikaze.'

Blair perfectly articulated why the woke mentality is so alienating to most voters: 'People do not like their country, their flag or their history being disrespected,' he said. 'The left always gets confused by this sentiment and assume this means people support everything their country has done or think all their history is sacrosanct. They don't. But they query imposing the thinking of today on the practices of yesterday; they're suspicious that behind the agenda of many of the culture warriors on the left lies an ideology they find alien and extreme; and they're instinctively brilliant at distinguishing between the sentiment and the movement.

Blair concluded: 'The correct course for progressives on culture questions is to make a virtue of reason and moderation. To be intolerant of intolerance – saying you can disagree without denouncing. To seek unity. To eschew gesture politics and slogans. And when they're accused of being insufficiently supportive of the causes – which is inevitable – to stand up for themselves and make it clear they're not going to be bullied or pushed around. This will lose some votes among a minority with loud voices; but it will bind the solid but often silent centre to them.'

Oh how the political earthquake in Washington DC has proved both of us right!

The way Trump won back the presidency, after what many – including me – believed to be the career-ending debacle of 6 January, reminded me of a conversation we had for British *GQ* magazine back in 2008, when the world was deep into a devastating economic crisis, about how he had survived the last big financial crash in the early 90s.

He told me then: 'I owed billions and billions of dollars, and nearly went under. Many of my friends went under. It was a very tough time. But I reacted positively. I went forward quite bravely, I'd say, given that so many people were going out of business. My theme was "survive till '95" and that turned out to be about right, because those who survived until then were OK. I learned I could handle pressure. A lot of my friends couldn't and just took the gas. I knew tough guys, or people who I thought were tough but who crawled into a corner, who put their thumbs in their mouths and cried, "Mummy, I want to go home." I didn't lose sleep, I never, ever gave up, and I fought hard to survive.'

Say what you like about Trump, but it's impossible not to admire his extraordinary thick skin, and ability to soak up the kind of pressure that would, and has, irrevocably destroyed many other people. He repeatedly walks directly into the fire and then right back out on the other side.

The phrase 'man up' could have been invented for Trump, which is ironic given that the woke brigade wants anyone who uses that phrase to be cancelled. I know, because whenever I've used it, they've tried.

Apparently, it's the worst possible thing to say to anyone feeling pressure or anxiety, because it implies the only way to be a real man is to have a stiff upper lip, roll your sleeves up, and suffer.

But I don't think that.

I agree it's important for men to talk about their problems and express their emotions if they want to.

However, that shouldn't preclude men from doing things the Trump way too.

When he got shot, many of us would have curled up into a terrified ball on the floor, crying like a baby, and waited for the Secret Service.

Instead, he wrestled himself back to his feet, his face splattered in blood from his bullet-grazed ear, thrust his fist high in the air, and shouted, 'FIGHT! FIGHT! FIGHT!'

At that moment, Trump had no idea if the shooter had been neutralised, or if there was another shooter in the crowd.

He acted purely on instinct.

And those instincts were to fight.

Trump showed astonishing personal courage that day. And I think the iconic defiant image of him was another big factor in why he won the election.

Americans didn't have to like him to instinctively admire his fortitude under fire, and to believe he would fight for them too.

And it spoke to a wider belief I have that the world's gone too bloody soft.

Since the emergence of social media and smartphones, as Jonathan Haidt explains in his brilliant book *The Anxious Generation*, many young people's brains have become increasingly scrambled by constant, and mostly negative, dopamine rushes that have rendered them incapable of dealing with the real world.

If there's one thing I would love to infect these youngsters with, it's not cripplingly self-pitying wokery, which does so much to fuel victimhood and self-pity, but determined confidence.

Again, you don't have to like Donald Trump to recognise that he has extraordinary self-belief.

However tough the challenge, he always backs himself to succeed.

I love that quality.

The week after Trump survived the would-be assassin's bullet at the rally in Pennsylvania, his doctor revealed the

AR-15 semi-automatic rifle bullet that grazed his right ear was a quarter of an inch from entering his head and killing him.

Trump called me after seeing me discuss it on TV and we had the most profound conversation we've ever had.

'How are you?' I asked.

'I'm great,' he replied, 'considering I got shot last week.'

He made it sound as casual as going to the dentist.

'I'm so glad you survived,' I said.

'Me too!' he laughed, again. 'Those bullets were whis-tling past my head, making a big wooshing sound. The shooter was a good shot – apparently, he was a hunter. Fortunately, I turned my head at the right moment which saved me. I guess God was looking out for me. Kinda crazy, right? But there was so much blood from my ear! I never knew ears bleed the most of any part of the body, so that was an interesting discovery.'

That night, he'd been back on stage at another rally in Michigan, standing alone and exposed in front of 20,000 strangers. Not many public figures would have risked that so soon after nearly being assassinated.

'Were you not apprehensive about going back out tonight?' I asked.

'I couldn't let myself think about that,' he replied. 'I had to get straight back out there, or I might never have. I don't want to get yippy.'

The yips are what all performers, from sportsmen and singers to comedians and politicians, most dread – a sudden 'mental block' inability to do what they do, sometimes triggered by a traumatic event that instils a chronic anxiety or fear.

This was a surprisingly vulnerable response but very revealing too.

Trump knew he couldn't let himself admit to any self-doubt in case it consumed him.

We chatted for 20 minutes that night, just seven days after he cheated death, and I'd never heard him sound so self-reflective or oddly serene. Here was a man who knew he'd been given a miraculous second chance at life.

'This is why I believe in God,' he said. 'There's nothing more important than good health, Piers. Stay healthy, OK?'

As Winston Churchill, who fought in several wars, once said: 'Nothing in life is so exhilarating as to be shot at without result.'

Victimhood is another woke scourge that the world would do well to see the back of. Every time I see someone getting the victim card out over some pathetically trivial and often wildly exaggerated and embellished thing, I think of my oldest village mate Miles Caldwell who died a horrible death in 2024 from incurable glioblastoma brain cancer aged just 58, without ever uttering a single word of self-pity from the moment of his diagnosis, which came out of the blue, to his passing 15 months later.

Compare and contrast with *Empire* actor Jussie Smollett, a lying, narcissistic, deluded, fame-hungry, self-piteous imbecile sentenced to 150 days in jail after inventing a vicious homophobic race attack on himself by two white Trump supporters in Make America Great Again (MAGA) caps.

In fact, it was two Nigerian-American men he had paid $3,500 to enact the fake attack.

When rumours began circulating that the story might not be entirely what it seemed, indignant Smollett doubled down by saying that if his attackers were Mexicans, Muslims, or black people, 'the doubters would have supported me much more ... and that says a lot about the place that we are in [in] our country right now'.

In fact, it was Smollett's disgraceful plot to make himself the victim of a staged attack that said a lot about the place America, and the world, was now in.

In one final repulsive moment in court, Smollett defiantly raised one hand, Mandela-esque, to the sky and bellowed theatrically: 'If I did this, then it means I stuck my fist in the fears of black Americans in this country for over 400 years and the fears of the LGBT community.'

Well, yes, you repulsive little twerp, that's EXACTLY what you did!

In fact, it's hard to think of a more sickening affront to civil and gay rights than Smollett's great fat lie. Or a more insidious example of what the woke mind virus can do to a once-normal person. We must never surrender to it ever again, for sanity's sake.

In fact what THIS book is about is how vital it is that we never let such a freedom-slaying virus infect our minds again.

It's the story of how fanatics chipped away at men, women, language, advertisements, history, movies, politics and universities until their bullying tactics – such as glueing themselves to roads – sparked an almighty common-sense uprising.

It's also about the personal qualities I feel we all need to combat and reject wokeism, many of which – whether you like the guy or not – Donald Trump has in spades. These include resilience, determination, a strong work ethic, an unashamed preference for winning over losing, a fighting spirit, and speaking one's mind without fear.

PART TWO
TURNING THE TIDE

A mass uprising of common sense is rapidly reshaping politics, media and the way we all think about free speech. I would love to say my last book was the key tipping point, but it might have had a bit to do with pandemic-induced mania. That was the moment at which woke appeared to be at the very height of its powers, perhaps even with us forever, but it was actually the catalyst for its spectacular demise.

Woke thinking was baked into the systems that govern and entertain, becoming an omnipresent irritant, until the dam finally burst. A sudden flood of common sense is now washing over us with spectacular force and speed.

Chapter 4

UNWRECKING PEOPLE'S LIVES

I don't need my tea to be a moral compass or political advisor.

'Trans women are not women,' ran the splash headline across multiple front pages as the UK's Supreme Court ruled that a woman is only someone born female. Not long ago our Prime Minister censured women in his own party for putting it less starkly, after babbling incoherently that '99.9 per cent of women do not have a penis'.

BBC newsreader Martine Croxall's bold correction of 'pregnant people' to 'women' live on air – marked with an eyeroll and palpable scoff – would previously have caused outrage. But the BBC received just one formal complaint for this insolence towards imaginary pregnant men and it was speedily dismissed.

In America, Facebook launched a global free-speech project with Donald Trump: a man whose speech it used to deem too dangerous to allow him an account. Quite recently vaccine sceptics were banned from travelling and risked losing their jobs. Now one of them runs the US Health Department. Fat was fabulous, until the Danes invented Ozempic. Now celebrities are all rakishly thin again and everybody seems very body-positive about it.

The speed and force of this total volte-face has been so head-spinning that, until recently, it would have had a trigger warning. As abruptly as the Blair-and-Britpop nineties ended with the terror-and-twitter noughties, we can now look back on the period 2015–2025 as *The Wokies*. A crazed decade in which initially well-meaning worries about sexism and racism morphed into tyrannical purity purges and a campaign to remake every aspect of society, language and culture.

Children were no longer born as baby girls or boys but as blank canvasses for 'gender-creative parenting', which *Time Magazine* said would 'eliminate oppression'. Persistent flirting and chivalry were held in the same contempt as sexual violence and prosecuted not by judges but self-appointed jurors on Twitter. Bigotry was to be assumed at all times and punished pre-emptively because, as one influential academic paper explained, 'Black Lives Matter, and Yes, You are Racist'. Video games were no longer to blame for the perennial crisis of violence, laziness and moral decay. Now it was 'cisgender white males'.

Undoubtedly I am a straight white man but so is Harry Styles and we have very little in common. That's the inherent flaw with lumping everybody into identity groups defined by their characteristics instead of their character. The woke mindset filed us all into boxes marked 'victim' or 'villain' and used the same logic to justify authoritarian correction treatments like restricting speech, rejecting science and discrimination by race and gender. Any threat to this virtuous new regimen had to be stamped out by any means necessary.

The endless hunt for victims and victimisers meant outrage often wrecked even the good deeds. The world's top YouTuber Mr Beast, who creates ingenious challenges, stunts and game shows, sponsored 1,000 cataract surgeries for the visually impaired and captured their reactions as they opened their newly functioning eyes for the first time. But the big story was a controversy about his 'performative altruism', as *USA Today* put it, while BuzzFeed News huffed that he 'seems to regard disability as something that needs to be solved'. Surely, we all do?

True believers were always a noisy minority, but they ruled like a theocratic dictatorship with an iron grip on the flow of information. Media, movies, politicians, advertisers, celebrities and universities were in lockstep with the new commandments. There was a whole vocabulary for recruiting supporters and punishing dissent. After all, nobody wants to be a 'privileged, victim-shaming transphobe on the wrong side of history' (which could make a good headline for the *Guardian's* review of this book, if it bothers writing one).

The whole thing felt like a substitute religion for people who are ironically often proud of their atheism. It was a way of gaining moral superiority and a shared purpose. It had a strict and judgemental moral code that didn't allow any deviations, which is how you get 'Gays for Gaza' and puberty blockers for kids in the same ideology.

And it tried to impose its morality on everybody else through shaming, with people like me cast as the blasphemous sinners.

It's suddenly very easy to roll our eyes about it all, as Maxine Croxall did on the BBC. There's a reason people say 'one day we'll look back at this and laugh' at a moment of crisis. But it wasn't very funny at the time. Wokeness wrecked people's lives.

Careers and reputations were shattered by the 'guilty until proven innocent' outrage machine. Women's rights to private services were shattered to accommodate men who said they were women. These times felt like a hopeless regression into a demoralising state of relentless, joyless conflict. We were sliding into a black hole of bad ideas which so many people instinctively knew to be outrageous but were afraid of the consequences of saying so. We forgot how to be civil and how to respectfully disagree and it made everybody more anxious and miserable.

The whole woke doctrine was divisive, damaging and frankly demented. It might have carried on a lot longer if it wasn't for a series of seismic shocks that began with the pandemic in 2020. If you're puzzled about why so many people suddenly seem to be free speech warriors who despise the mainstream media, and how President Trump just rose from the political ashes, it actually all started there.

That wretched cycle of lockdowns and sourdough aptly coincided with the high peak of the woke mind virus – a highly contagious brain fog that causes blindness to progress and different points of view. Social media gave everyone the opportunity to voice an opinion, unleashing a vile torrent of pent-up anger. It had a captive audience. Everything and everyone was online. The tribal and identity-obsessed bubble of braying opinions was the only place for most of us to interact with other human beings, who were all looking for attention or causes. Now there were urgent new reasons why proving you were the very best person – and your enemies the absolute worst – felt existentially important.

Opportunities for howling opprobrium were everywhere. Every day a hapless figure was publicly shamed for boarding a train without a mask and thereby condemning a cadre of grannies to certain death. We were bored, worried, irritated and consuming nothing but online squabbles and endless dreadful news about the relentless march of Covid. It was too easy to make outraged scapegoats of unwitting twerps who seemed to be prolonging the misery for everybody else. Cancel culture dialled up to eleven.

Admittedly, I did a bit of this myself. I won a lot of plaudits on *Good Morning Britain* for holding British ministers to account for reckless incompetence and cack-handed cover-ups. Many other broadcasters were stuck in a Blitz spirit-type funk, in which criticising the government was treated as a threat to national security.

What I now regret is later turning my considerable ire on regular people, people who had legitimate grievances about vaccine mandates or prescient questions about official narratives. I still think I was right, but I was uncompromising and unwilling to listen to people who thought I was wrong. You might even say I got a bit woke about it all.

I was rallying for a rapid end to the misery and tedium and saw anybody getting in the way of that as an inconsiderate bollard. I implicitly trusted scientists when they insisted vaccines would actively prevent the spread of the virus, which they ultimately didn't, and I was overly censorious of people who vaunted their refusal to take them.

It will always be my opinion that the jabs were a miracle of modern science and they have demonstrably saved many lives. But clearly the official line on transmission was overstated, as was the 'wet market' origin story whose detractors were silenced as anti-China racists. I'd treat the official lines with a bit more suspicion if it ever happened again, as a journalist should.

It may disappoint the thousands of trolls who still hammer me for this online every day, but I wasn't the big problem. Real censorship exploded during the pandemic. A lot of people had already become far too comfortable with the idea that bad opinions or bad people should be socially ostracised. Now the powerbrokers were doing it industrially. The word 'misinformation' turned up everywhere as a way of toxifying anything transgressive and it quickly became a powerful political weapon for discrediting opponents.

Facebook and YouTube quickly blocked content that questioned the efficacy of face masks, even though officials had initially done so themselves to protect dwindling supplies for health workers. It was a bannable offence to claim the coronavirus had leaked from a world-renowned Wuhan laboratory that literally makes and studies coronaviruses. Now the US government, among others, says that is most likely what happened.

Stifling contrarian ideas only ever creates suspicion and mistrust, especially when the apparent heresy later turns out to be true. Nobody had really thought very much about the incredible power of liberal-minded tech bros in Silicon Valley to police ideas and information until that point. It was a lightbulb moment for me and I quickly started noticing that censorship was mutating like the virus itself.

The *New York Post* published a jaw-dropping report on the contents of a laptop owned and then abandoned by Hunter Biden, the Democrat leader's son. It contained vivid evidence of his influence-peddling, dodgy business dealings and drug use. All of the major social media platforms decided to suppress it, just weeks before the 2020 presidential election.

Facebook CEO Mark Zuckerberg later told Joe Rogan they banned people from sharing the story because of secret FBI warnings that it could be Russian misinformation: a false line parroted by 50 former intelligence officials who signed a letter demanding the media ignore the story.

They were emphatically wrong and they probably always knew it. Sure enough, evidence on the laptop was used in tax fraud charges to which Hunter pleaded guilty four years later, and it was shown to the Delaware jury that convicted him of gun felonies.

As I said at the time, there isn't a snowball's chance in hell they would have closed ranks if the story was about one of Donald Trump's sons. CNN cancelled a long-scheduled interview they'd been pestering me for when I accused the US media of behaving like partisan hacks for choosing not to investigate it at all.

Almost every major broadcaster in the US repeated the Russian meddling story and apparently saw nothing alarming about social media platforms uniting to bury a political bombshell on the eve of an election. It felt normal because we'd put them in charge of protecting us and we initially had no better option than trusting the government. Censoring bad information seemed justified in the panicked early race to save lives, but it was a can of worms.

I'm sure they later felt justified in kicking Trump off social media altogether once the precedent was set. Most platforms banned the President and many of his followers for inciting and supporting the appalling 6 January riots but continued to host accounts run by the Kremlin, the Chinese Communist Party and the holocaust-denying Ayatollah of Iran. Apple, Amazon and Google deleted the right-wing platform Parler from their app stores.

All this did was inflame the long-term decline in media trust and fuel a ravenous appetite for free speech. Conservative opinions and anti-government conspiracy theories became a forbidden fruit online, where provocateurs have always thrived, and there was growing weariness in the 'can't say that' sensibilities of cancel culture. Millions more people went searching for alternative opinions and sources, and they never came back.

A complete lack of trust in any information or each other is desperately unhealthy. Democracy is the competition of ideas and solutions based on a shared set of facts, but increasingly we can't agree on what the facts are. If a new pandemic began tearing across the world tomorrow morning, I have serious doubts about many people's readiness to believe it was real, which is a dangerous situation to be in.

George Floyd's shocking murder came smack bang in the middle of the pandemic's first peak and Black Lives Matter sailed into a perfect storm. This was the single most significant moment of overreach in the so-called culture wars and the most potent stimulus for the backlash. BLM became MeToo on steroids. It was the zenith of moral absolutism, with zany and reactionary ideas adopted zealously by brands, governments and the media until many fair-minded people got fed up. It has changed the world, just not in the way it originally intended.

Let me be very clear, the murder was sickening. I watched the full video for the first time in open-mouthed horror, shouting aloud as vile cop Derek Chauvin ignored Floyd's repeated pleas for mercy. TV networks across the world played it repeatedly at the exact moment there was nothing for most people to do besides watch the news and get mad about it online. I supported the people who first poured on to the streets in grief and anger because atrocities warrant a reaction. But the reaction became an overreaction, and some people went stark raving mad.

For a brief moment there was unity, but it didn't last very long. Initially peaceful demonstrations quickly descended into mob rule with violent occupations in public squares and reckless vandalism. At least 19 people died, 14,000 were arrested and riots caused more than $1 billion in property damage in what became the biggest civil unrest in US history. TV viewers who were appalled by this carnage – many still obeying stay-at-home orders – were told they just didn't get it. This was a justified expression of centuries of pent-up rage.

The mass media's coverage of the BLM riots dealt a significant blow to its credibility, especially among US conservatives. Even now, clips from that time are circulated to discredit news brands and reporters as biased fanatics. MSNBC anchor Ali Velshi is still mocked for his reporting on riots in Minneapolis, where Floyd was killed, for assuring viewers they were 'not, generally speaking, unruly' while standing in front of a raging inferno lit by arsonists.

The *New York Times Daily* podcast carefully used passive phrasing like 'and there were fires that were set' rather than simply 'violent protesters set buildings on fire'. CNN crossed live to a reporter standing in what looked like a scene from *Mad Max* with a headline banner that cheerfully declared: 'Fiery but mostly peaceful protests after police shooting'. That's a bit like saying 'Funeral, but most royals still alive after Queen's death'. Protesters rewarded this pandering by attacking CNN's headquarters in Atlanta.

Violence never justifies more violence, as most sensible people would agree. But many influential people were straining every sinew to signal that *they* understood the pain. Common sense and neutrality were completely thrown to the woke wolves.

An essay in *New York* magazine explained: 'The entire journalistic framing of "objectivity" and political neutrality is structured around white supremacy.' Of course it isn't! Being objective means not allowing your feelings to cloud your judgement of facts.

The term 'white supremacy' appeared in more than 8,000 articles that year. This extreme, racist and rare belief that white people are born superior was suddenly being presented as a fact of life and a crime we could all be guilty of. For everything else there was 'white privilege'. I'd barely heard the phrase before BLM went berserk, but suddenly everything was white privileged.

A massive debate erupted on Twitter about whether Anne Frank had white privilege. Yes, the 13-year-old Jewish girl who hid from Nazis in a loft for two years before being dragged off to die in a concentration camp. Apparently she had white privilege because at least her family was able to hide for a while. It may be the stupidest argument I've ever heard – in an extremely crowded contest. Few people were feeling privileged as they sat locked in their kitchens for a year, whether they were black, white or screaming violet.

People were cancelled for the most pathetic reasons in the stampede of frenzied outrage. It was now impossible to be woke enough. The chairman of the US Poetry Foundation released a statement denouncing 'systemic racism' and pledging 'solidarity with the Black community'. He was forced to resign a few days later because the statement was too short. Poets signed an open letter saying: 'Given the stakes, which equate to no less than genocide against Black people, the watery vagaries of this statement are, ultimately, a violence.'

Big brands were also terrified of being accused of complicity and duly went bonkers. Many poured millions of dollars into Black Lives Matter but were still chastened for tokenism. Huge companies like Barclays, Deloitte and Budweiser started outbidding each other with ever more outlandish plans to create limitless jobs open only to black people.

Uncle Ben's Rice abolished its 74-year-old logo of a smiling elderly black chef due to its 'inequities' and parent company Mars announced $4.5 million in donations for black chefs – even though they had just summarily fired Uncle Ben himself, the world's most beloved black chef. The global market for Diversity, Equity and Inclusion (DEI) – payrolled bureaucrats who enforce diversity quotas and racial sensitivity training – went ballistic.

These businesses were petrified of being tagged as 'institutionally racist' or failing to 'meet the moment', but they quickly began alienating the quiet majority, neither racist nor activist, who were just wondering what the hell was happening.

Yorkshire Tea was being praised on social media for keeping quiet and getting on with the important business of making tea bags, prompting them to hastily clarify they had merely been 'taking some time to educate ourselves' and that BLM's critics should never buy their tea again.

My view is that very white tea and very black tea are both equally wrong and any colour-based debate involving tea should be strictly limited to how it should be properly brewed (precisely four minutes' stewing by teapot or 23 anti-clockwise stirs for robust strength, added to a mug with half an inch of milk in it). I don't need my tea to be a moral compass or political advisor.

For a while, everything had to be racist. British MPs debated a report on why our countryside – the actual fields and forests – is 'racist and colonial'. The England and Wales Cricket Board (ECB) commissioned an investigation into itself, which duly ruled that cricket is institutionally racist too. The only acceptable opinion was that racism is everywhere and that everything was broken.

US protests turned into the ludicrous 'de-fund the police' movement. The idea was to eradicate police altogether on the basis that some police are racists, even as carnage raged on the streets. None of the de-funders ever had a good answer to the question of who else they would call if a maniac was battering down their back door. Liberal darlings including Alexandria Ocasio-Cortez and incoming vice-president Kamala Harris preposterously supported them.

And then came the statues. US protesters beheaded or toppled monuments of Confederate leaders like Stonewall Jackson and Robert E. Lee while tributes to presidents Washington, Jefferson, Theodore Roosevelt and Grant met an undignified end. Christopher Columbus, one of the first Europeans to travel to the Americas, was hauled from his plinth.

A statue of Edward Colston, the British merchant and philanthropist whose riches were made in the evil slave trade, was ceremonially dragged through the streets of Bristol and dumped into the harbour. London's famous Parliament Square statue of Sir Winston Churchill was shamefully defaced and then even more shamefully shrouded in a giant metal box before the next demonstration.

Churchill's leadership and resolve in rallying Britain to repel the Nazis is a major part of why protesters still have the freedom to march in this country at all. By today's enlightened standards Churchill also did some terrible things and had some awful views, but that doesn't negate his indelible role in saving our entire way of life.

Ransacking the past to score points in the present became a powerful tactic in the woke playbook. It helped tell their miserable story about how our countries and power bases have always been irredeemably evil. Historian Lynn Hunt wrote a warning about 'presentism' 23 years ago. It's the warping of history by infusing it with very modern issues like identity politics, and if you know what to look for, it's suddenly visible everywhere.

A professor named James Sweet wrote a very scholarly criticism about 'presentism' and inaccuracies in the *New York Times'* '1619 Project', which 'aims to reframe the country's history by placing the consequences of slavery ... at the very centre of our national narrative'. If you start off with a conclusion like that then it's not really history any more; it's selective moralising which is only based on a true story. Sweet was hectored into a grovelling mea culpa.

Police don't issue speeding tickets to people who, many years ago, drove at 40mph on a road where the speed limit has now been reduced to 20mph. But we are all supposed to pretend that everybody in the past should have been as perfect as we are. Great authors like Charles Dickens, Roald Dahl and even George Orwell have been targeted by this time-travelling morality tardis, which condemns opinions or behaviours that sound alarming today but were banal at the time.

My overwhelming feeling at that miserable moment was that we were becoming hooked on wallowing. Bombarded with reasons to believe that nothing had ever been worse and that people had never been so awful. Now that we're enlightened and know everything, we're doubly evil for putting up with an imperfect world.

At the apex of the handwringing, actor and comedian Kevin Hart told a magazine we were living through 'white power and white privilege at an all-time high'. Polls in the US and UK showed that concerns about racism and prejudice had hit their highest ever point.

Was racism really at its worst? Was 'white power' at its all-time high? Higher than when British lodging houses displayed signs reading 'no blacks, no Irish, no dogs'? Higher than when black people were appallingly segregated in public spaces or literally enslaved?

It's just wrong. There are still racists in Britain, and in the US, but we call them out. They're on the margins of society because we instinctively know they're bad people. We've made enormous strides forward on so many of the social issues that were supposedly at crisis points. Women have equal rights enshrined in law. Gay marriage has been legalised and normalised across the Western world and the gay pride flag has flown over the White House.

We should feel good about the fact that our society is getting better and fairer. We should celebrate progress. It shouldn't have to be a coin toss between preemptively declaring 'mission accomplished' and insisting that racism and sexism are at epidemic levels on every corner of every street. Wokeness burned itself out by projecting a miserable, dystopian version of humanity that the vast majority of us do not recognise.

Six months after the BLM riots there were atrocious scenes at the US Capitol as pro-Trump protesters stormed the seat of US democracy over his false claims the election had been rigged. I watched in horror as poorly prepared and poorly equipped police were overwhelmed by a fired-up mob, and I've never held back in condemning what I felt were appalling scenes that shamed America. That hasn't always done me any favours, as I discovered while sitting across the desk from a visibly seething Trump at Mar-a-Lago in March 2022.

The reason this subject still rankles with Trump and his supporters, five years later, is the sense of institutionalised hypocrisy. A double standard that says woke radicals are protected by a moral halo but anybody else who steps out of line is a threat to our way of life.

The 6 January attack on the US Capitol led to nearly 1,600 federal charges with 5,000 FBI staff executing the biggest criminal probe in US history. Felony convictions led to severe jail sentences, including 22 years for an organiser who wasn't actually there and five-year jail terms for non-violent trespassers. It was rarely out of the news for the next four years. And the whole narrative was framed by President Biden's infamous 2022 national address in which he railed angrily against 'MAGA Republicans' (aka just over a quarter of all voters) for threatening 'the very soul of this country'.

In the case of the BLM riots, the vast majority of charges were dropped. Some shocking high-profile cases, such as a Portland protester who beat an innocent bystander unconscious, were handled at local level and ended with much lighter punishments. More than 2,000 police were injured nationwide and a small-town police chief was shot dead by looters. But US cities and police departments ended up paying $80 million in settlements to protesters who combined forces to sue them for infringing *their* rights.

Trump pardoned all of the 6 January rioters in one of the first acts of his second presidency. It felt like settling scores. I'd probably have agreed with the chorus of criticism from Democrats, especially about the release of prisoners who'd been violent, if Biden hadn't shattered their moral high ground by doling out pardons to his own family.

You don't have to agree with the comparison between 6 January and BLM, devoid of many nuances, to understand how it was galvanising for Trump's base. It followed the familiar pattern of one-sided retribution.

Justin Trudeau, the wokest world leader in history, unleashed hell on truckers protesting against his vaccine mandate. Emergency wartime powers were invoked, leading to shocking scenes of police batonning protesters and assaulting journalists. Banks were ordered to freeze the protesters' accounts and any businesses supporting them were visited by police.

Trudeau, who was leader of the Liberal Party, remember, told a TV station that his vaccine-hesitant critics were 'often misogynistic, also often racist'. I've often teased wokies about their embrace of fascist tactics they profess to loathe but here was the self-styled nicest guy in politics proving my point. 'This leads us, as a leader and as a country, to make a choice,' he said. '*Do we tolerate these people?*'

The whole point about democracy, and the whole problem with woke illiberalism, is that we have to 'tolerate' people whether we agree with them or not.

Many fair-minded people have been repelled by this double standard. We've lost our grip on right and wrong in the clamour to support our tribes. The institutions that govern us and frame our whole culture buckled under the pressures of wokery and repeatedly made it clear which side they were on. They prioritised ideology over duty and fear over facts – sometimes with devastating consequences.

The UK grooming scandal is an important example of where it can lead – and why facts matter. Thousands of mostly white young girls in the Midlands and north of England were groomed and abused by organised groups of men, who were mostly of Pakistani heritage. Authorities grotesquely covered up both the scale and the nature of the abuse.

They put concerns about inflaming racial tensions – and a fear of being accused of racism themselves – over their fundamental duty to protect the most vulnerable. It's bitterly ironic that many of these vile men were themselves driven by an abhorrent and racist belief that white girls were less moral or less valuable than girls in their own community.

We know all of this because some journalists and some public figures, working closely with whistleblowers and victims, bravely grasped the nettle. Investigative journalist Andrew Norfolk, who sadly died this year, first reported on the scandal in a front-page splash for *The Times* way back in 2011. But they were fighting against a tide. Far more energy was expended on the cover-up than the coverage.

At very high levels it was decided that the gory details of a genuine scandal would shatter the narrative about a successful multicultural society. Channel 4 shelved a documentary on it to avoid aiding the racist British National Party in local elections. A senior police officer in Rotherham, where many of these atrocious crimes took place, told a victim's father that the 'town would erupt' if the details leaked out. Many victims were abused for years because of this culture of conspiracy and fear. It's unforgivable – and it can never happen again.

The Prime Minister's belated decision to commission a full national inquiry is the first step to making sure of that. Very little has actually been done with the findings of the previous investigations. None of the 20 recommendations of the initial independent inquiry have been implemented, three years after they were published. It only became a global news story this year because it came to the attention of Elon Musk, who used his platform X to amplify horrific details, which many people may otherwise never have known.

That's where Tommy Robinson comes in. Most people know my views on Tommy Robinson. He has a string of criminal convictions for violence, fraud and contempt of court. I also think he has a long record of brazen race-baiting and, in my opinion, an obvious prejudice against Muslims. But that doesn't mean that he is wrong about literally everything and, whatever his motives, he has been raising the grooming scandal in lurid terms for a long time.

What Elon Musk and his followers get wrong is the idea that Robinson is a martyr who was recently jailed for telling the truth. He was sent to prison for contempt of court in a case that had absolutely nothing to do with blowing the whistle on grooming gangs. But many in the US now seem to believe he is a beacon of truth who has been pivotal in exposing this evil.

I think the exact opposite is true. He's so toxic and discredited in the UK that he's been hung out deliberately as a sacrificial lamb by people who would rather not talk about the very uncomfortable facts of the case. It's easier to persuade most people that it's not an issue they should dwell on if it's labelled as a Tommy Robinson issue.

The same smearing tactic has been used repeatedly to shut down important and honest discussions about divisive woke hobby horses, like teaching kids about gender spectrums and racial oppression. Parents who complained were just dismissed as Fox News-watching dogmatists.

Too many people in positions of power and influence went along with the idea that wokeness was indisputably on the right side of history. And if you're so laser-focused on the certainty of your own virtue it becomes morally justifiable to do almost anything to get your way. The legacy media is certainly guilty of this and it has played a large part in its own downfall, particularly in the US.

Just look at the extraordinary attempts to cover up President Joe Biden's infirmity. Biden's physical and cognitive decline was probably visible from space. It was certainly visible over 3,500 miles away in London, from where I wrote regular columns for the *New York Post* and the *Sun* about the pitiful spectacle of an octogenarian commander-in-chief who could sometimes barely string a sentence together.

Age ravages us all – but not with the same speed or severity. My friend Dame Joan Collins is 92 but has the energy and zest for life of someone half her age. And as I said on my show when Mick Jagger joined Biden at age 80 – one can't get no satisfaction, the other can't get up the stairs.

Many in the US media had convinced themselves so fundamentally that they were the good guys – that Trump was so deeply threatening to their vision for a virtuous world – that anything which could benefit him was indefensible. They went to enormous lengths to disguise Biden's obvious collapse and insult anybody who exposed it because it felt morally justified.

Then-CNN media correspondent Oliver Darcy accused conservative commentators of 'desperately pushing conspiracy theories' about Biden's senility. NBC News talked of a 'conspiracy theory that Biden won't be on the ballot ... centred largely on the thought that Biden is too old'. A cavalcade of brass-necked Democrats went unchallenged as they told TV audiences he was as 'sharp as a tack', 'a strategic thinker at the top of his game' and that 'this version of Biden is the best ever'.

Biden's Press Secretary Karine Jean-Pierre, who comically claimed on several occasions that she 'couldn't keep up with' the ailing president, tried to discredit videos of him wandering listlessly off stage and forgetting names as 'cheap fakes'. Deep fakes are AI-generated videos of celebrities saying or doing embarrassing things. 'Cheap fakes' were real videos of the president saying or doing embarrassing things that the White House did not like.

It all came crashing down at the CNN presidential debate. A global audience collectively gasped as the president constantly trailed off mid-sentence and often looked painfully confused. The whole game was up. Biden's friend and donor George Clooney twisted the knife by scolding Democrat dementia-deniers who now needed to 'stop telling us that 51 million people didn't see what we just saw'. Democrats circled the wagons to oust the president and the rest, like Kamala Harris, is now history.

President Biden's announcement in May 2025 that he'd been diagnosed with aggressive prostate cancer, which some experts believe he may have had for several years, sadly only underscores the point that he was completely unfit for office. The sick glee with which the news was celebrated by some US conservatives shows how hateful and tribal our politics have become.

CNN's Jake Tapper, who co-hosted the now-infamous debate, published a jaw-dropping book with journalist Alex Thompson on the cover-up. It details how Biden didn't even recognise George Clooney and repeatedly forgot the names of his closest and longest-serving aides. It's desperately sad, but it's also a shameful scandal, one which Tapper told me may be judged by history as 'worse than Watergate'.

Chuck Todd, former host of NBC's *Meet the Press*, made a candid appearance on *Uncensored* this year in which he acknowledged the 'fear that some members of the media had that they would be perceived as helping Trump if they somehow diminished Biden'. He also said that censoring Trump and many of his supporters after 6 January was a 'fundamental mistake', which drove many into a powerful and rebellious new media ecosystem.

The British media is saintly by comparison, but we have our own milder experiences of moralising agendas that ended up riling audiences. I voted against Brexit, for example, and think it has been a demonstrable disaster. But it was clearly caused in part by scornful experts and smug pundits who said worries about immigration and sovereignty were just bigoted.

The BBC can't help but choose and report stories that appeal to mostly liberal-minded middle-class people in cities because that is who they are. Reports on polarising issues like transgender rights have always been delivered with an obvious underlying assumption that everyone at home is on board with it all – or should be. Our TV news is not politically partisan in the way it is in America, but it still has that dated sense of self-appointed duty; we'll be the judge of what you should know.

Independent thinkers like Joe Rogan have completely smashed this system. Tens of millions of people watch and listen to a show that is based entirely on freewheeling longform conversations with interesting people.

Rogan has built a colossal global audience by sharing unedited interviews with authors, comedians, celebrities, scientists and many controversial characters shunned by the traditional media's judgemental selection process. The only barrier to entry is whether he is interested in what they have to say. Inevitably, he gets a lot of blowback for choosing to 'platform' the wrong people or failing to eviscerate them for inaccuracies, but that misses the point of why people love what he does. Rogan is a comedian and a skilled conversationalist, not an interrogator. He dignifies his audience with the intelligence to make up their own minds and do their own research about what his guests say.

Good reporting matters and we still need it. Most journalists care deeply about accuracy and investigate without any agenda. But increasingly it just fails to satisfy the rapacious new appetite for free speech and the curiosity about ideas and opinions that challenge mainstream thinking.

Covid's big bang of censorship and suspicion only turbocharged the mass movement to a product people find more authentic and more interesting. The decisive role played by 'anti-woke' podcasters, including Rogan, in the US election was probably the final nail in the coffin for the old systems of influence in the legacy media.

Rogan's Trump interview and his surprise subsequent endorsement were a big splash in a race everybody said was too close to call. Anybody who doubts that should remember Trump's victory speech, in which he tipped his hat to the 'mighty and powerful Joe Rogan'.

Trump sat for three hours on Rogan's show; airily discussing everything from whale psychology to regrets, tariffs, aliens and what he told Kim Jong-un ('You're always building nuclear ... why don't you go take it easy? Go to the beach, relax.') Left-wing networks like MSNBC had been pumping out 24/7 warnings on how Trump was the new Hitler, but he reached more voters in one fascinating podcast than they do in a year.

Rogan also issued an open invitation to Kamala Harris, whose campaign staff offered a measly one-hour interview and insisted Rogan fly to New York to do it – which he never does for any of his guests. They had a list of off-limits topics and were squabbling internally about how the woke activist base would react to her mingling with someone who – gasp – opposes trans athletes in women's sport.

Meanwhile Trump made a much-ridiculed tour of 'bro' podcasters, which endeared him to millions more people. He laughed about psychedelic drugs with Lex Fridman, showed a sincere interest in Theo Von's past drug addiction and entertained Andrew Schulz about his 'weaving' style of hitting dozens of topics in reply to a single question. TV stations were screaming to vanishing audiences about an evil dictator while millions more voters were watching him bantering with their favourite podcasters and generally coming off as a decent guy.

Election campaigns will never be the same again. Trump's youngest child Barron reportedly urged his dad to embrace digital media over stuffy network interviews and it was astoundingly good advice. The powerbase has now shifted almost entirely from legacy media brands to podcasters and influencers deemed more trustworthy and more genuine.

The media's post-election inquest launched a thousand columns and panel debates about how 'the left needs a Joe Rogan'. But they already had one – it was Joe Rogan. He endorsed Bernie Sanders for the 2020 election and speaks up for solidly left-wing ideas like socialised healthcare, universal basic income and free university for all. He often whacks Trump when he thinks he's getting it wrong. Like most of us, he just can't be stuffed into a polarising box labelled MAGA or Democrat, Conservative or Labour, Oppressor or Oppressed. And he can't stand woke!

Journalism 'watchdog' Media Matters, which has seemingly only just been connected to the internet, released a worrisome survey of the most influential online voices in the wake of Trump's victory. It warned of an 'overwhelming' right-wing bias in this dangerous new space.

Among those inked in MAGA red were Rogan, Dr Phil, Lex Fridman and me. The *Guardian* has similarly labelled like-minded podcasters 'Fox News for young people'. In reality many of the people cited by Media Matters, as well as me, are independent-minded people who rejected the uncompromising lunacy and censorship of the mad left and found ever-growing audiences who felt the same.

And what short memories they have. Until very recently the internet writ large was not very kind to actual conservatives. Twitter was famously a seething hotbed of virtue-signalling and liberal views until Elon Musk took over and turned it into X. Supposedly incendiary accounts, which again included mine, used to be secretly limited to stop them adding new followers. Users are now evenly split between Democrats and Republicans, according to Pew Research Center, whereas it used to be weighted 65 per cent to the left.

It's also a fact that you are now far more likely to see offensive speech, outrageous images and outlandish conspiracy theories. My personal view is that some of it, like Kanye West's vile antisemitic tirades, has no place on any platform. But none of the people yelping about this seem to recognise that all of it has been driven by a massive backlash to a very recent time when censorship reigned with impunity.

Chapter 5

CALLING OUT THE BULLSHITTERS

It's not 'far-right' to prefer that your daughter isn't knocked about by a formerly-male athlete ...

It's a fact that Arsenal have never won the Champions League but, as painful as that is to me, I don't want to live on a social media timeline where everybody talks about a famous victory that never actually happened to make me feel better. Equally, I find the London rain depressing, but I don't need the weatherman telling me it's sunny to spare my feelings. We've had enough of people telling us the sky is green and the grass is blue because their argument only works if the whole world is upside down.

Recounting all of this is almost as wearying as living through it, but it's essential for understanding the ferocity of the backlash that is now underway. After years of creeping illiberalism, cancel culture, identity politics, woke media bias, man-bashing and wallowing, the pandemic created optimal conditions for the worst excesses of woke-ness to flourish in a meteoric blaze of virtue-signalling. But it also became a decisive tipping point, beyond which a silenced majority decided enough was enough. Politics and media across the Western world have now been turned upside down and inside out.

President Trump's improbable comeback is the totem of this mass repudiation, but he is not the only beneficiary. Crowd-pleasing populists are taking advantage of a tectonic vibe shift all over the place. Reform UK, led by treacherous weasel and skilled politician Nigel Farage, came from nowhere to win 14 per cent of the national vote in Britain's general election and wiped the floor with everybody in the May 2025 local elections.

Alternative for Germany (AfD) staggeringly doubled its vote share to become the second biggest party in a country that has long-shunned the far right over the shame of its Nazi past. Nationalists won elections in Austria and the Netherlands while surging in Spain and Sweden. National Rally leader Marine Le Pen looked a racing certainty to become France's next president before she was banned from running over embezzlement charges; a move which may still charge her rise if she spins its echoes of 'lawfare' against Trump.

Not long ago all of these movements were considered untouchable extremists and most commentators interpret their recent success as a dangerous global slide towards autocracy. If that's the case, their opponents need to urgently get a grip on why it's happening and move rapidly to the common-sense middle ground.

Yes, some of the populists' voters are likely to be crazed bigots and racists. Many are simply turning up their noses at the woke-liberal package deal, which is usually bundled with patronising alarmism and the defence of a status quo that people feel isn't working for them.

Kamala Harris branded Donald Trump a 'fascist' as Democrats pivoted their ailing campaign to increasingly hysterical claims that democracy was in peril. People just didn't buy it. A similar story played out in Argentina where dire warnings about 'the world's latest fascist wannabe' did nothing to impede Javier Milei, who is currently proving to be pragmatic and relatively popular as the reformist president.

The ascendant populists have all moved cannily into the vacant common-sense lane. They may well have sinister motives, but their public positions are popular because they sound like things normal people think. They all argue that unchecked mass migration has disrupted societies and that countries need strong borders. They each believe there are two sexes – male and female – and that this is a biological fact. They've noticed that constant browbeating for historical sins has demoralised people and that patriotism doesn't have to mean racism.

None of that is fascistic terror. And none of it would have been remotely out of place in a Bill Clinton speech during his two terms as a popular Democrat president. If the new nationalists are as terrifying as the left says they are, it needs to get serious about appealing to real people again instead of crusading for imaginary victims.

Most people are not far-right or far-left, they are neither racist nor activist, and they don't particularly care about other people's sex lives as long as it doesn't involve them. That's where I am and where I'll always be. The politicians who claim to speak for this common-sense majority are going to keep on winning.

Left-wing politics has always been a big tent for the classical liberals and democratic socialists with a few seats at the back for hardcore progressives. But the lunatics took over the asylum – and most people don't consider themselves to be lunatics.

Way back in 2019, Barack Obama warned his party: 'The average American doesn't think that we have to completely tear down the system and remake it. There are a lot of persuadable voters, and a lot of Democrats, who just want to see things make sense. They just don't want to see crazy stuff.' He hit the nail on the head. But the party he once led went all-in on the crazy stuff at the very moment everybody was sick of it.

Their rap sheet of lunacy could fill a book on its own. California's Democrats effectively legalised shoplifting below $950, which is why you now have to ring a bell and wait for an employee to unlock the shampoo shelf at a pharmacy. A wave of 'progressive prosecutors' in liberal states went soft on crime on the basis that justice is unfair on minorities. Biden's disastrous open border policy led to a record 10 million illegal crossings: the equivalent of everybody in London turning up and needing work, shelter and security.

Democrats pushed divisive 'critical race theory' in schools. Instead of celebrating the fact that all humans are equal, it teaches that black children are 'oppressed' and that white children are their 'oppressors'. Progressive lawmakers Cori Bush and Jamaal Bowman tabled legislation demanding $14 trillion in reparations for black Americans as compensation for historic slavery, at the exact moment inflation and the cost-of-living crisis were at their pocket-burning peak. For some reason neither of them retained their seats in Congress.

President Biden condemned Republican state governors as 'close to sinful' for trying to ban transgender surgeries on children, even though most voters of all allegiances believe it should be illegal. Kamala Harris is on record, in a 2019 questionnaire, as being prepared to support taxpayer-funded sex changes for illegal immigrants.

Democrats who spoke out against trans athletes wrecking women's sports were threatened with expulsion. Most people think all of this is completely nuts. It's not 'far-right' to prefer that your daughter isn't knocked about by a formerly-male athlete or to believe in things like going to prison for crimes and paying for shampoo.

I've always considered myself to be a liberal because liberalism meant free speech, free markets, small government, a colour-blind society and a general but pragmatic aversion to war. Yes to all of that. But the woke-branded liberalism is the polar opposite.

In the US, Democrats have become the preaching party of censorship, red tape regulation and seeing everything as racially charged. Now it's Republicans who are deeply suspicious of big government institutions like the CIA and ferociously defensive of free speech and meritocracy. The always-offended Democrats campaigned with a big rod up their backsides while Trump riffed like a stand-up comedian and made MAGA the anti-war movement.

In surrendering their movement to the crazies, Democrats have become everything they once loathed. Conservative headbangers used to be the ones on talk shows preaching morality and demanding obscene TV shows or movies be banned. Now liberals are the condemnatory fun police, cancelling celebrities who are not unimpeachably woke and finding outrage in things like edgy comedy. It's no surprise they are losing the working-class people they claim to exist for.

Shortly after Trump's victory I interviewed James Carville, a legendary Democratic strategist who propelled Bill Clinton to the White House with the victorious catch-phrase: 'It's the economy, stupid.' It was a blistering maxim for the simple idea that winning involves doing what voters care most about, not what you think they should care most about.

'It's just idiotic,' he said of the woke takeover. 'There are principles liberals tend to share. We look at people as individuals, not part of a larger group. We try to help people who are trying to make it as opposed to people who have it made. This was a very loud part of the party that really came to rise after the murder of George Floyd. They thought it had given them a licence to be stupid.'

That licence has now been revoked and chopped into pieces. Trump won emphatically with a kind of anti-establishment coalition of common sense. He was arguably both a cause AND an effect, carried over the line by many of the apparently oppressed minorities that

Democrats claimed to be rescuing. Trump made huge inroads with Latino voters, female voters, young voters and even black voters, all of whom Democrats have long taken for granted and expected to flock to Kamala Harris in droves.

Trump was also the first Republican in six decades to win with the lowest-income working-class voters and a comfortable majority of what pollsters sometimes rudely call 'the poorly educated'. His top team includes multiple former liberals, including dynastic Democrat Robert F. Kennedy Jnr and former Democratic presidential challenger Tulsi Gabbard, who quit the left over its 'woke ideologues' and 'cabal of elitist warmongers'.

Elon Musk, the world's richest man and Trump's biggest donor in the 2024 election, is a former centrist Democrat who used to be the pin-up model of environmentalism (Al Gore looks even worse in Speedos). That particular bromance ended in public infamy, but there's no denying Musk's hefty contribution to putting Trump back in the White House.

Undoubtedly, Trump is a one-off political force of nature, but he's not alone in providing a common-sense refuge for disenchanted working people. The surging populists in Europe have all eaten the left's lunch. Recent polls show Reform UK have more working-class supporters than Labour.

It's not all because of woke, obviously. Every country has its own basket of grievances and its own basket cases in government. But pick almost anywhere on the map and you will hear the same complaints about progressive elites in wealthy cities who campaign for weirdo minority causes while traditional communities are throttled.

Van Jones, a progressive black lawyer and former advisor to Obama, summarised it perfectly: 'When you're defending the status quo, you're going to lose. [And] you're offending most people in the country; calling everybody sexist and racist and homophobic and every other name – then saying "please follow us". If progressives have a politics that says all white people are racist, all men are toxic and all billionaires are evil, it's kind of hard to keep them on your side. If you're chasing people out of the party, you can't be mad when they leave.'

In 2024, Britain elected its first Labour government for 14 years in a landslide. On the surface that would seem to buck a trend, but this was no Marxist revolution. Sir Keir Starmer spent four years surgically detaching the party from his predecessor Jeremy Corbyn: a curmudgeonly elder socialist in the Bernie Sanders mould who refused 15 times in 15 minutes to call Hamas 'terrorists' in his only *Uncensored* interview.

Tony Blair, Labour's most successful ever leader, urged Starmer to reject identity politics and speak for centrist Brits 'who want fair treatment for all and an end to prejudice, but distrust and dislike the cancel culture, woke mentality'.

It took him a painfully long time but, eventually, Starmer listened. Labour won by promising to be the party of 'wealth creation' with no tax rises, cuts to welfare and a populist 'smash the gangs' slogan on illegal migrants. They are yet to deliver on those promises, but after years of cringeworthy question-dodging, Starmer spoke out against teaching 'gender ideology' in schools and allowed his talented Health Secretary Wes Streeting to clarify: 'Men have penises, women have vaginas. Here ends my biology lesson.'

Starmer also very quickly cosied up to Trump with the offer of another royal pomp-laden state visit. He tried to reckon with the president's controversial tariffs by declaring: 'The world has changed, globalisation is over.' The PM is pictured so often with a Union Jack that even venerable news magazine *The Economist* has reported on his 'flag-shagging, the uncouth vernacular for overt displays of patriotism'. Bill Clinton gave some very Blair-like advice to the Harris campaign about indulging trans issues and fearmongering instead of clear common-sense messaging, but he was assured it was no big deal.

Voters repeatedly say otherwise! Every new president loses their campaign trail gloss when it becomes clear they won't in fact do everything to please everybody all of the time. Trump's trade war and performative threats to annex Greenland quickly turned off many moderates and divided even his hardcore MAGA base, many of whom were also deeply opposed to his decision to bomb Iran's nuclear facilities.

And his fumbling over releasing the court files on paedophile Jeffrey Epstein became a political crisis. High-profile stories about mismanaged migrant deportations took some of the gloss off his remarkable and extremely popular measures to rapidly toughen up the US border.

But there was resounding public approval for his opening barrage of executive orders, which Trump had memorably unveiled as 'a revolution of common sense'.

Biologically male athletes were banned from women's sport. The endless spectrum of self-selected genders was cut to simply 'man' and 'woman'. Schools were ordered to stop teaching kids that racism is embedded in everything. Federal funding was cut for child transgender surgeries. Racial quotas introduced under the banner of diversity, equality and inclusion (DEI) were abolished across the government in favour of a 'colour-blind and merit-based society'.

Only woke fanatics can answer the question of why it took a right-wing and white president to restore Martin Luther King's aspiration of character over colour. Everybody should have equal opportunities, no matter their sex or race. But DEI meant hiring specifically because of sex or race; creating unequal opportunities to manufacture a utopia.

In practice this has generally had the effect of dragging everyone down to the same lower level rather than building everybody up. And it's hard to square it with the American dream of rising or falling on your own merits in a system that judges what you do, not what you are.

Devastating wildfires ripped through Los Angeles in January 2025, causing hundreds of billions in damages and burning thousands of homes to ashes. They came, literally, very close to home for me and I know several people who lost properties they've cherished for many years.

As the local government and fire department came under increasing scrutiny for snags and delays, an interview clip surfaced of the deputy fire chief Kristine Larson celebrating all of her DEI policies. Not coincidentally, she had earlier been gleefully unveiled as the first black lesbian to ever hold the role.

'You want to see somebody that responds to your house … that looks like you,' she said. 'It gives that person a little more ease.' I think I speak for everyone when I say that if my house is on fire and I am trapped inside it, I am extravagantly uninterested in your sexual preferences or your physical appearance. I just want you to get me the hell out of there.

Unfortunately, Chief Larson isn't confident about being able to do that – and she thinks it's my fault. Recounting some familiar questions posed by DEI critics, she said: '"Is she strong enough to do this?" Or "you couldn't carry my husband out of a fire". To which my response is "he got himself in the wrong place if I have to carry him out of a fire!"'

The point about DEI is not that women, black people or gay people are unfit to be firefighters. It's about a systematic misjudgement of priorities in which identity is of equal or greater importance than ability.

There are many black gay women who are far more useful in a fire than me, but I want that to be the reason they are there. Not that they are more 'marginalised' than I am based on the institutional oppression index. And if you are someone who now leaps on *every* black public figure as a 'DEI hire', you are part of the problem too. The identity obsession works both ways and does nothing but drive us apart.

Not long ago, most big companies would have shrieked in protest about Trump's dismantling of DEI. Instead, they generally agreed it wasn't working as intended and that all employees ought to be treated equally again. Google, Meta, Amazon, Pepsi, McDonald's, Walmart and many others dropped their DEI programmes. Some businesses in the UK quickly followed suit. At that point Trump's approval records hit a record high spanning both of his terms. If only wars and trade deficits were as easy to unravel as wokery.

Trump's common-sense shock therapy happily coincided with a global spring clean. It felt like the woke cobwebs were being blasted away everywhere. Justin Trudeau's demise was a timely and hugely enjoyable coincidence.

He was finally forced to quit as Canadian Prime Minister after nine years as the self-appointed High Priest of Woke, who preached a lot and practised very little. He will surely be remembered as the most PC-crazed world leader in the history of peoplekind, as he once insisted we rename it. And few people on earth have better personified the moral sanctimony and shameless hypocrisy of the whole mentality he espoused.

Not only did Trudeau tank the economy with ridiculous initiatives like a 'gender-neutral budget', a detested fuel tax and billions spent on 'gender initiatives' in faraway countries, he was repeatedly caught with his virtue-signalling trousers around his ankles. Most infamously he was exposed for wearing blackface to an *Aladdin* gala at a private school – where he was not a clueless young pupil but a 29-year-old teacher.

Pressed on whether this was a one-off, Trudeau conceded he'd also painted his face black to play singer and civil rights campaigner Harry Belafonte at a talent show. And when photos quickly surfaced of a third blackface outing, he confessed it may have happened so many times that he simply couldn't remember.

Trudeau's *Arabian Nights* became a hallmark case of cancel culture's one-way traffic and why it has now been so resoundingly exposed. Before the Trudeau scandal erupted, Megyn Kelly was forced out of NBC for musing on her show that it used to be normal to wear blackface in the US tradition of dressing-up as celebrities on Halloween. She never did it herself, nor did she say it was OK, she just pointed out the big shift in social attitudes as part of a roundtable discussion.

Kelly even issued a tearful on-screen apology as celebrities and outraged social media users demanded her head on a platter – but it wasn't enough. She had to go. Her real crime was that she is an anti-woke conservative who used to be on Fox News and had never been forgiven. CNN's Don Lemon scolded: 'They knew exactly what they were getting when they hired Megyn Kelly,' while uncharitably chiding that she was now 'suffering the consequences' of her own mistakes.

Justin Trudeau's own apology, which was for actually wearing blackface himself and doing it so often it boggled his memory, got a decidedly more welcoming response. He tapped all the right notes on the virtue-signalling xylophone: 'discrimination', 'understanding', 'hurt', 'I come from a place of privilege ...'

This time Don Lemon was bowled over with clemency. 'When someone apologises – wow!' he gushed. 'We don't often see that here. A world leader who is saying "I should have known better and I'm sorry." You could go about that however you want. But to me, that does mean a lot.'

Trudeau refused to resign that time and was roundly praised for his sincerity in what many supporters and columnists called a 'teachable moment'. He narrowly won the next election, condemning us to several more years of nauseating social media posts like: 'People across the country are lighting candles to honour Indigenous women, girls, and 2SLGBTQQIA+ people ...' In Trudeau's Canada, falling asleep on your keyboard was apparently a gender.

Most people are now very happy to admit they're glad to see the back of all this. Many of the formerly wokest Democrats in the US are now rushing to pretend they thought it was foolish all along. The last decade has not been a happy one for society. Layer upon layer of bonkers ideas were imposed on a lot of people who wanted nothing to do with them, reinforced by politics, media, culture and education. In each case the bad ideas have been painstakingly unpicked by a critical mass of resistance or unravelled by their own hypocrisies.

It hasn't been easy. A lot of people risked or in some cases sacrificed their careers and reputations in defence of common sense. The bonkers ideas weren't as much of a problem as the methods used to enforce them. We have to relearn how to debate ideas and disagree with each other without attacking like rabid dogs and savaging all our opponents.

The fact we can get two starkly different interpretations of reality based on who we follow, watch or listen to is proof that competing opinions are of vital importance. How can you be sure that you are right if you have never heard an explanation of why you could be wrong?

The big tech companies may now be bending to the will of the new president on free speech but I have no confidence they'll maintain these newfound principles when the political winds are blowing in the opposite direction. It will take sustained pressure and vigilance from us – the people whose data and attention they profit from. And some governments are still finding censorship a difficult habit to kick.

In the UK, police now make a staggering number of arrests for posts on social media. The total rose by 58 per cent between 2019 and 2023 to 12,183. We've seen scandalous cases like that of childminder Lucy Connolly, who was handed a 31-month jail sentence for inciting racial hatred over a post on X she deleted and apologised for. Connolly had been enraged by viral content falsely claiming a horrific child stabbing in Southport had been perpetrated by one of the tens of thousands of illegal immigrants living in British hotels and posted: 'Mass deportation now, set fire to all the fucking hotels full of the bastards for all I care … if that makes me racist so be it.'

It was unquestionably racist and deeply offensive. But was it actual incitement worthy of more than two years in jail? It wasn't a call to action at a specific facility but an opinion, however vile it may have been, as underscored by the 'for all I care'. Authorities were working overtime to quell social tensions after the appalling child murders but they overreached. I worry deeply that we've forgotten what free speech is and why it matters.

A big reaction is very often followed by a big overreaction. Protests about George Floyd were a reaction. Rebuilding society around the idea that every man, woman and beast is a horrible racist was an overreaction. Now we've come to our senses we need to be wary of overreacting again in totally the opposite direction.

A few months ago I hosted a heated debate on my show about the absurdity of two massive fundraising campaigns in the US for distinctly unworthy causes. One was for a black teenager who was accused of murdering his classmate (as opposed to his victims' family). The other for a white mother who called a five-year-old child the n-word for apparently teasing her son at the park.

I was totally gobsmacked when a panellist defending the racist mother's free speech brazenly admitted to using the n-word herself, whenever she feels like it. 'You're entitled to do it,' I told her. 'And I am entitled to call you a despicable racist.' There is a middle ground between condemning everybody as unspeakably racist and glorifying actual racism in response. We all need to stay on it.

It should be possible to criticise or even loathe President Trump without declaring him the new Hitler and condemning all of his supporters as dangerous democracy-ravaging bigots. Just as it should have been possible to prefer a Democrat for president without pretending Joe Biden was a Mensa-leading intellect and a prize fighter.

Social media isn't helping with any of this, but it isn't going anywhere and it's not going to get any better. There is no shortage of very persuasive people trying to drag us with them to the extreme fringes because winning at all costs is the aim of their game. The best defence is to trust your instincts and stay with the common-sense core in the middle. That means calling out bullshit no matter which direction it comes from.

This particular culture war is coming to an end after a bruising battle. It will turn out to be a battle fought in vain if we allow one set of uncompromising, censorious crusaders to be replaced by another who do exactly the same things from the opposite side. In the spirit of humility, I suppose the logical conclusion is that everyone should try to be a bit more like me.

Chapter 6

MASCULINITY

We used to have Bruce Willis and Jean-Claude Van Damme; now we have Timothée Chalamet and Paul Mescal.

The Netflix series *Adolescence* is a dark, gritty and frankly boring British drama about a 13-year-old boy who kills a schoolgirl after being radicalised by toxic masculinity. Viewers are catapulted into a hostile teenage world of always-online boys with malevolent expectations of girls and hapless adults whose children have been hopelessly corrupted by influencers like Andrew Tate. Protagonist Jamie stabs a female classmate for spurning his romantic advances and teasing him for being an 'incel' – a familiar online slur for young men who can't attract women.

It's not unusual for me to be bored stiff by a series that is hailed as a masterpiece by critical decree, or cynical about a work of fiction that is lauded for its clunky moralising of real-world social issues. But the nauseating universal reverence for *Adolescence* was in a league of its own. And ironically, the hysterical mandatory acclaim for its fundamentally demoralising message is exactly the kind of thing that fuelled the toxic culture it warns us about.

'Netflix hit proves necessity of male role models' boomed a headline on the BBC News website, one of many that overlooked the fact that it's a completely fictional story. 'How *Adolescence* is making Britain face up to toxic masculinity,' gushed the *Guardian*. Prime Minister Sir Keir Starmer praised the series in Parliament before welcoming its creators to Downing Street and announcing that *Adolescence* would be shown in all secondary schools across the country. MPs convened a special committee to ask its writers for insights into the warped minds of their imaginary characters.

Conservative leader Kemi Badenoch was harangued in a testy *BBC Breakfast* TV interview for revealing she hadn't watched the show. 'It's a fictional series, not a documentary,' she protested, 'let's talk about what's real.' The visibly offended presenters took turns grilling her on whether she stood by what she'd just said, as if she had accidentally confessed to a murder herself. It felt like we were one short step away from having to show *Adolescence* passports to prove we could safely mingle in restaurants and stadiums.

Starmer spoke about 'abhorrent violence' that is 'carried out by young men, influenced by what they see online' as a crisis needing urgent attention. Nobody would argue that radical misogynistic violence in schools isn't a problem worth worrying about – but only to the extent that it actually exists. Britain has vastly bigger issues with gang-related stabbings, especially in London where black teenagers are killing each other at truly disturbing and tragic levels. Where is the smash-hit series with compulsory viewing and the national inquiry about that? Where was Starmer's urgency about the child grooming scandal, which was covered up and kicked into the long grass year after year?

The logic behind forcing children to watch *Adolescence* is that they will be shocked into heeding its dire warnings and fixing their wicked ways before it's too late. Repeated references to 'manosphere' figures like Andrew Tate are supposed to resonate with their seminal relevance. But really it's just an updated re-telling of the same downbeat story that has dominated culture throughout the woke years. Girls should be instinctively fearful of boys, whose primal beastliness is an inevitable and grave threat. It's also a fundamental misunderstanding of teenage boys, who would be a lot more likely to reject Andrew Tate if Keir Starmer told them he was a 'Top G'.

Andrew Tate is the most infamous and prolific of the machismo online influencers. He racked up a staggering 14 billion views on TikTok before eventually being banned from the platform for his misogynistic views. At one point he was one of the most-googled men on planet earth. Tate's success has spawned a vast network of acolytes and imitators who spew misogynistic bile to generate clicks and attention from mostly male followers. They offer simple answers to complicated questions and have skilfully upended the narrative that masculinity is something to be ashamed of.

Psychologist Dr Jordan Peterson, who is certainly no fan of Andrew Tate, tore into the prime minister's 'posturing' in a scintillating interview on my show. 'It's oriented not to help young people but to make Mr Starmer feel a hell of a lot more secure in the idiot assumptions of his dimwit progressivism,' he said. 'It's exactly what you'd expect from the progressive playbook. We're going to double down on the incels! Why don't you give some thought to figuring out why they're so bloody isolated? How about 60 years of radically demoralising, quasi-feminist, dimwit hedonistic leftist propaganda shovelled at them from grade one all the way through university!'

I don't suppose Jordan will be watching the second series – and I think he has a point. I'm not denying there is a massive problem with vile misogyny, which is increasingly plastered all over social media. I just think young men are surrounded by it already and in my experience they are mostly smart enough to recognise it for what it is and never repeat it in the real world. They are also in desperate need of a more positive message. The eternally virtuous find it very easy to be shocked and appalled by Andrew Tate but far harder to admit they are part of the reason he became so popular in the first place.

Wokeness sees men as undeserving champions who need to be knocked off their perch to make room for everybody else. Young men have duly been downtrodden and browbeaten for years by a society and media that systematically chides them for exploiting women, even as their status has begun to terminally decline. They are bombarded with reasons to feel bad about themselves from the moment they are old enough to kick a ball, if indeed they are predictably boorish enough to want to do that instead of choosing to play with a doll instead.

Boys are raised to expect that they will inevitably become greedy men who dominate boardrooms and profit from the 'gender pay gap'. Even middling success in a menial role is probably at the expense of a woman who never got the chance.

The male-dominated manual jobs they have toiled in for generations are not respectable or desirable any more. They should sit still and slog through an academic system that has been redesigned to benefit almost everybody other than them. Teachers, politicians and experts glibly demonise their inherently ghastly traits while Hollywood movies mock their buffoonery and celebrate their defeat by the ubiquitous and flawless girlboss.

Popular podcaster Chris Williamson holds the rare distinction of being a former *Love Island* reality TV star who is also highly intelligent and interesting. He prepared an illuminating list of genuine news headlines about problems, trends and world events blamed on 'toxic masculinity' and read it aloud in an interview on my show: 'Gang violence, climate change, the financial crisis, Brexit, the election of Donald Trump, not wearing a face mask, eating meat, physical fitness, fast food, capitalism *and* communism, hip hop, smelling of Axe body spray, being stoic, risk-taking, religion but also secularism and atheism, playing board games, being interested in cars, and saying "hello" or "have a nice day" ... all terrible examples of toxic masculinity.' It's no wonder we are exhausted.

While all of this has been happening, men have quietly and guiltily receded into the gutter. The stats are devastating. Men are four times more likely to commit suicide – and the disparity is getting worse. Boys are more likely to be kicked out of school for bad behaviour, more likely to drop out due to poor grades, and more likely to end up in jail. In the US only 3 out of 10 valedictorians – the best-in-class academic champions of high school – are boys. There will soon be two girls for every male graduate at university in the UK.

Young women in full-time work in the UK actually now earn almost 9 per cent *more* than young men, meaning the so-called gender pay gap has flipped, and it only levels off when they have children. White working-class boys in Britain have the worst outcomes and lowest expectations by almost every available metric, even though the entire system has been rigged for helping every demographic other than theirs.

Adolescence gave lots of pompous people an opportunity to clutch their pearls about male issues but the main message was, again, that males *are* the issue. Boys are primitive receptacles for poisonous misogynistic messaging by malevolent men, whose combined villainy is destructive and damaging for victimised women.

Under this mindset, boys are always the problem and never the solution. Yes, it's a sad fact that some boys grow up to be appalling men who perpetrate the vast majority of all domestic violence – and worse. But we are more conscious of this than we've ever been and the lion's share of men are repulsed by it. The relentless societal focus on only the bad guys has become a bitterly ambition-sapping, spirit-crushing pill for young men to swallow, especially as they find themselves failing in a world they were always told was unfairly weighted in their favour. That is precisely why so many have taken the so-called 'red pill' instead.

I've interviewed Andrew Tate several times in the past few years, including in Romania where Andrew and his brother Tristan spent four months in jail awaiting trial for serious criminal charges they deny. Since our most recent interview, both brothers have been told they face a raft of extremely serious charges in the UK, including rape, actual bodily harm and human trafficking, and an extradition warrant that will be enforced when the Romanian charges are resolved.

Each time I've interviewed him, including long before this wave of serious charges, there has been a controversy over whether I should 'give him a platform'. In my view this is a delusional and dated way of pretending he would just disappear if only it wasn't for me. The fact is that he speaks uninterrupted to millions of people on his own platforms, every day of the week. At least on my show he gets interrogated and a reality check for his most extreme views.

More young guys stop me in the street to ask about Andrew Tate than anybody I have ever interviewed. Given that my list includes several US presidents and Cristiano Ronaldo, I think that tells a story in itself.

If 'brand' Tate is all performance art and he has a secret cuddly and reflective persona, I have yet to see any evidence of it. In person Tate is sharp, suspicious, intensely focused, belligerently confident and always in the highest gear.

He's the centre of gravity in any room he walks into and capable of being disarmingly charming. I can understand why people are drawn to him. But that doesn't mean he's not simply weaponising his grasp of serious problems that undeniably exist for his own monetary gain.

In Tate's world, classically male traits are not dangerous or shameful but are the essential foundations for lavish success. He sells a beguiling action-packed lifestyle of private jets, fast cars and big cigars with a compulsive dedication to fitness and a gleeful glorification of profit.

Mental health woes on Planet Tate are obliterated by exercising, socialising and succeeding. Men can take charge of their own destiny – attracting women and accumulating great wealth – with relentless discipline, fortitude and perseverance. Failure is your own responsibility, not everybody else's, and being weak is, in fact, a weakness.

It's obviously all very cartoonish, and clearly there are plenty of valid reasons to consider Tate an extremely dangerous messenger, but the fact is there is nothing wrong with any of *that* part of his message. There's also a reason why it sounds good to many young men who have for so long been told that all of these intrinsic desires are repugnant and that they should strive to be precisely the opposite.

The most absurd by-product of the vital MeToo movement was the enforced feminisation of men in popular culture as a remedy for 'toxic masculinity'. There ought to have been a middle ground between expecting men to repress all of their feelings and eulogising us for vaunting our vulnerabilities and getting pedicures.

Hulking, sulking, indomitable action heroes like Rocky Balboa, Dirty Harry and *Die Hard's* John McClane gave way to an anxiety-ridden Spider-Man and an emasculated James Bond who just wants to sit and talk about his feelings. We used to have Bruce Willis and Jean-Claude Van Damme; now we have Timothée Chalamet and Paul Mescal. In the US, Boy Scouts are now 'Scouting America', lest they are imbued with ghastly boyish sins. Action Man has roller blades and a water pistol instead of military hardware.

This insidious indoctrination has been gradually building to a climax for many years now. I'll never be able to forget the time when a load of gurning male celebrities including Benedict Cumberbatch, Tom Hiddleston and Joseph Gordon-Levitt vaunted their virtues by wearing scruffy T-shirts with 'This is what a feminist looks like' emblazoned on them. The trend only fizzled out when Nick Clegg and Ed Miliband joined in, which is surely enough to make even the most rabid feminists extinguish their flaming brassieres.

Running alongside all of this was persistent hectoring on how male and female traits are simply hammered into us by an old-fashioned society of fossilised dinosaurs. Boys and girls are really just a big soupy broth of gender fluidity, waiting to be poured into a bowl of their own choosing.

I have three sons and a daughter. My siblings have eight girls and a boy between them. I can tell you, as any parent can, that girls and boys are different. They think and behave differently, they experience emotions differently and they mature differently. But it's become offensive to say it.

No matter how many times we are sent to the naughty step for our natural urges, men are just not buying it. We are competitive, risk-taking and adventurous. Most of us are attracted to beautiful women and like to think we have a shot with all of them. We are ambitious and we want to make money because for thousands of years we have been hunter-gatherers or breadwinners whose natural aggression is of life-and-death importance for the people we most want to protect.

That inherent sense of purpose is what drives a lot of us to get out of bed in the morning and kick ass. Remove it at your peril. Feminists and man-bun metrosexuals may sneer about 'Big Dick Energy' but it sometimes comes in handy when we need men to fight in wars, build a house or squash a spider – often when they'd rather be doing just about anything else.

Where Andrew Tate and his clones lose me is with their demeaning of women. A wretched subset of the so-called 'manosphere' pushes the noxious idea that defending masculinity means asserting male superiority. Celebrating men suddenly lapses into bullying women. I have grilled Tate on his extreme, dangerous and frankly ridiculous positions, such as claiming women should 'bear some responsibility' for sexual assault and that women are male 'property' who must 'obey'.

There is no justification for calling women 'bitches' and 'hoes' or boasting about violence towards women, all of which he has done too many times to count.

You can't complain about chivalry being ludicrously condemned as sexist, as I do, and then treat women with vulgar disrespect. It completely defeats the point. Radical feminist types have tried in vain to poison gentlemanly gestures like holding doors, carrying heavy bags or paying for dinner as some kind of patriarchal power play. They are no such thing. They're a well-mannered expression of a man's respect for a woman – and most women appreciate it. The world needs more gentlemen, not fewer, and for me it's a big part of what real masculinity is.

Another manosphere-manufactured problem young men are grappling with is grossly distorted expectations about women. The idea that stunning women will inevitably swoon over men if only they follow a simple programme of domineering and chauvinism. The reality is that flirting, meeting and mingling – essential ingredients in the recipe for life – have reached a nadir. And pretending to be an obnoxious machismo influencer is not likely to improve matters.

Years of chilling warnings about the myriad ways a man can make a woman feel uncomfortable have left many young men too afraid to talk to them, never mind charm them. And the mass migration of young people to dating apps has poured fuel on the flames.

Seducing a woman used to involve social skills and bravery. A man had to summon the courage to walk over to a woman in a bar, dazzle them with conversation or humour, and persuade them that they were worthy of an hour of their attention. Rejection was always a natural and healthy part of the process and it got easier to handle with a bit of practice, as many of us discovered with more regularity than we like to admit. Young people who were raised on participation trophies, mental health days and dating apps have no tolerance for genuine rejection because we've given them so many ways of hiding from it.

On a dating app the rejection is unseen and instantly forgotten. People just swipe compulsively through a meat market of faces and bodies; making instant judgements based solely on looks. Why risk real-world humiliation and awkwardness when you can just keep on swiping at home? I can see why it's easy but it's not how human beings are built to interact.

It's also a very unfair way to judge any man or woman, whose varied charms and complexities can't possibly be captured in a mugshot. How many women reading this book would honestly have 'swiped right' on their husband based only on a photo of his grinning chops?

More than a third of women say they have been approached less often by men since the MeToo movement, accelerating a long-term decline in personality-based pulling. About 60 per cent of young men haven't approached a woman in real life at all in the past year and – staggeringly – almost half of them never have in their entire lives.

Unsurprisingly, roughly the same number of young men are single – which is almost double the number of single young women, many of whom are simply dating older guys who actually have status and money.

Professor Scott Galloway, who has some devastating insights and invaluable advice on the masculinity crisis, says an average young man has to approvingly swipe on 1,000 different women to get a date with just one.

A tiny cadre of elite specimens – the 20 per cent of men with washboard abs, chiselled jaws and exciting jobs – get about 83 per cent of the swipes from women. Apps allow users to set strict filters, meaning a large number of women choose to never even see any men under 6 ft tall – immediately rendering 86 per cent of them literally invisible.

Women now judge men as briskly and brutally as I did a half-baked dance troupe on *Britain's Got Talent*, and I really can't blame them. They are fed the polar opposite storylines to the ones used to trample on men. For them the message is that they can do whatever they want to do and be who they want to be – which is laudable, until it reaches the part which involves erasing male involvement entirely.

Emma Raducanu fronted a preposterous HSBC campaign that rewrote fairytales as 'fairer tales'. Prince Charming was abolished and the strong independent princesses created their own successful businesses without any male involvement at all. I'm sure Raducanu felt proud of this pioneering assault on the glass ceiling but it was nothing new.

The celebration of female potential is now routinely bundled together with the complete erasure of men, as if one can't possibly succeed at the same time as the other. And if women are all courageous strivers who can 'have it all' without 'needing a (toxic) man in their lives', why on earth should they bother with the 80 per cent of men who look more like Tom Kerridge than Tom Cruise?

The grim result of all this is that men in their 20s are far more likely than women to be isolated, bored, sexually dormant and lonely. They age into unattached men in their 30s who are statistically at ever greater risk of lapsing into drug use and crime. Most men don't really want to be single, hence 'involuntarily celibate' or incel, and they find solace in online communities with similarly aggrieved boys who angrily blame women for denying them pleasure.

MeToo was an important and necessary movement. It brought global attention to the widespread issue of sexual harassment, domestic abuse and misconduct. But it moved on to terrifying all young men into thinking that expressing an interest in someone they're attracted to is automatically at high risk of being deemed predatory. There was a whole genre of books and a universal mindset about how women should make men work harder to win their affections. But at the same time we taught men that a second attempt makes them Harvey Weinstein. One third of couples used to meet at work but that number has plummeted because half of the office is at home on Zoom and the guys don't want to be reported to HR as creeps.

The whole notion of sexual energy has been stigmatised as a kind of companion to male harassment and violence. We have forgotten that it is mostly a very good thing. Men scale dizzying peaks when they find chemistry with a woman. Suddenly they become unstoppable machines with boundless energy and a wit sharp enough to slice concrete.

The impulse to go out and attract a partner is a massive motivation for men in all sorts of positive ways, including keeping fit and making money. It's driven by the very natural desire to make and protect new versions of ourselves, without which there would be no humans.

Young men haven't simply bottled up all of this desire and locked it away in the basement. They have mostly locked themselves away in the basement, where they are playing computer games and watching porn. About 30 per cent of all internet traffic is porn and 80 per cent of that is men looking for it and watching it. This is a ruinously vicious cycle that leads to more unrealistic expectations about women and what sex is really like, as well as snuffing out the healthy hunger to go and get it in real life.

If we don't rebalance our collective views on this very quickly it could get very bleak. Instead of teaching boys they are all inevitable born predators, trapped inside this hopeless world of toxic influencers, we should be teaching them how to approach women in *real life* with agency, confidence and respect. But we are fighting a rising tide. Most of the world's biggest and most ingenious companies spend most of their time convincing us that apps and screens can replace real human interaction. They can't.

Social media is really anti-social media because its whole mission is to replace eye contact with screen contact. A disturbing number of people already claim they're in love with AI chatbots, which are always available and never ask them to empty the bins. You can use your imagination about what will happen when lifelike humanoid robots are in widespread use.

Elon Musk talks a lot about population collapse as a greater threat to civilisation than climate change, whose fanatics have argued it's a good thing because there will be fewer people to trash the planet. That may be true but the effect on the billions of people still living on the planet will be devastating. Birth rates are plunging in many rich countries, leaving them without enough healthy young people to work and pay for the rising number of elders. South Korea, with a birth rate of 0.75 children per woman, has declared a national emergency and expects its work-force to shrink by 50 per cent in 50 years. It might be time to step away from the smartphone and try a bit of flirting again.

The only road out of this mire is paved with common sense and decent men who use it to offer constructive solutions. For every 'toxic male' misogynist there is an equally persuasive male influence with ideas worth listening to. Men like Chris Williamson, Steven Bartlett and Scott Galloway are able to cut through the woke insanity and the misogynist insanity at the same time, and there is now a reassuringly booming market for intelligent guys who can talk about fitness, discipline, money and confidence without the sinister woman-hating.

Dr Jordan Peterson, whose withering verdict on *Adolescence* I cited earlier, is one of them. He was accidentally catapulted to fame by calling out pronoun fascism but it was his thoughtful guidance for flailing young men that made him globally influential. His book *12 Rules for Life* sold more than 15 million copies. Peterson found his speaking tours were suddenly filling entire arenas, outside which he is greeted as a rockstar by grateful young men who have used his direction to turn their lives around.

I've interviewed Peterson plenty of times now on topics as varied as religion and Canadian politics. He has something forceful and incisive to say about almost everything, whether you agree with his politics or not.

Whenever we get on to the subject of masculinity he is overcome with emotion and often breaks down in tears. Peterson listens to thousands of young men, often bereft of role models, and finds himself on the frontlines of the crisis borne out by statistics I've talked about. They're often so listless and despairing that his simple lessons on things like responsibility, confidence and honesty are enough to make him a kind of surrogate dad.

'They have been programmatically demoralised,' he told me, fighting back tears, in a particularly emotional interview this year. 'I've seen that and it has been painful. And I am hurt by the observation that many of these young men can be set right with not much more than some truly encouraging words ... I've talked to more demoralised men in the past 10 years than probably anybody on the planet. I've seen what works. More demoralisation is not the answer.'

Peterson is regularly lumped in with characters like Andrew Tate in simplistic diatribes by woke merchants like the *Guardian*, which just shows the lack of understanding or compassion for young men and their plight in popular culture. Anybody who worries about and talks about men must automatically hate women. The reality is Peterson and Tate couldn't be more different.

Peterson's comments to me about Tate are worth repeating: 'I warned back in 2016 about this assault on masculinity. You think strong men are a problem? Wait until you produce weak men who are resentful and bitter because of their failures. You're going to see real trouble. And this is happening, to some extent, because Andrew Tate is one of the most popular influencers in the world.

'I wouldn't hold out much hope for the West if Andrew Tate is the direction that young men go in because he is a bad actor, right to the core. But if you're weak and dependent and demoralised by your culture, someone blustery and successful on the surface – aggressive and dominating in the power-mad way that he is – is going to look pretty damn attractive.'

He's right. Tate and the Tate-a-likes only exist as a bulwark against a culture that tells men their ambition is patriarchal and their desire is predatory. They can only be role models because the real role models have disappeared. The number of fatherless homes has rocketed in the UK and in the US. The long quest for female representation in male-dominated roles has totally ignored the vital importance of male representation in roles that have the biggest influence on young people. There are now more female military pilots, proportionally, than male nursery-school teachers and more than three-quarters of all UK teachers are women.

Every big industry has scores of helpful support groups for the sisters doing it for themselves, with names like Women in Banking, Association of Women Entrepreneurs and Asian Women in Business. And don't get me wrong, I think that's great. But maybe it's time to admit that men need a bit of help, too?

All of our support structures were created to address a real imbalance in society, but the balance has totally shifted now and we haven't reacted to it. We're still fixing a leak in the roof, even though the sun is shining and the room below it is on fire.

Any other marginalised group with the harrowing outcomes and litany of crises facing young men would be a top priority concern for woke crusaders. But they all got so stuck on the idea that men are the font of all evil, and mostly responsible for crushing all of the other oppressed groups, that they have simply been left to rot.

As with every aspect of wokery, we are witnessing the unintended consequences and massive backlash to punitive purges that began with perfectly good intentions. MeToo was a justified and overdue campaign to expose genuine high-powered predators and call time on serious male lechery. But it descended into preposterous trials by social media and men like Morgan Freeman, already aged 80 at the time, hauled over the cancellation coals for excessively flirtatious comments that were never close to criminal.

Feminism itself used to be about equal rights and equality, which everybody should support and most who are sensible did, until it became a campaign to proactively kneecap men. Feminists were riding high on their horses until trans came along; presenting an even more marginalised group for the woke to do battle for. Now feminists are blacklisted as oppressive trans-exclusionary radical feminists (TERFs).

This is the whole problem with turning the world into a zero-sum game. It should be possible to champion one cause without destroying the other, and that applies equally to man-bashing battleaxes and woman-hating knuckleheads.

Fembots will roll their eyes and say it's about time women had their turn on top after their centuries of suffering. But the young men of today had no part in any historic suppression of women and they very clearly are not reaping any benefits from it either. A rising tide should lift all boats, not leave half of them floundering underwater.

Love us or loathe us, the world needs men and men need masculinity. Whisper it under your patriarchal breath, but women quite like it too. We should be able to have difficult conversations about male violence and perversion without forgetting that a vast majority of men find it utterly reprehensible. Men need to step up too. If you don't like the new breed of boisterous male role models then try being a better one yourself. And look out for each other, because nobody is going to do it for you. That's the problem with living in the matriarchy.

Chapter 7

WHAT *IS* A WOMAN?

'I'm not sure I understand the question here.'

What is a woman? An adult human female. Easy. But not if you're part of the bloated class of pallid politicians and pandering public figures who have thrown women under the giant transgender bus in their own craven fear of the lunatic fringe.

It's a simple question with a simple answer. The repeated, squirming failure of a staggering number of political leaders to answer it would be hilarious if it wasn't so serious. Any hesitation is an instant admission that their loyalties lie with the movement that views both sexes as an optional identity-based mulch and will glibly sacrifice women's rights and separate spaces to prove it.

Being progressive used to mean fighting for women to have the same rights, the same opportunities and the same pay as men. Now it means fighting for the eradication of women as a concept. Somewhere along the way, lobbying for equal rights for transgender people turned into accepting that women's rights should be eroded in the process.

We reached the brink of a social disaster because of this cowardice. We are now successfully fighting back from that brink because of a formidable counter movement, led mostly by pissed-off middle-aged women who fought valiantly for the very rights that have insidiously been stolen back.

Three enormous developments in the past 18 months have shattered the dangerous mythology around the trans debate. First was the national NHS review of gender services by Dr Hilary Cass, which found gender-confused children were being hurried onto puberty blockers without any evidence they needed them and in many cases going on to regret it. The treatment is now only available for people aged 18 and above in the UK and many other countries have clamped down.

Second was President Trump's inauguration day declaration that only two genders can formally exist – male and female – which felt like a huge moment. A statement that would have got you banned from the internet and cancelled a couple of years ago was suddenly US law.

Third was the landmark ruling by the UK's Supreme Court that 'woman' and 'sex' can only refer to biological sex, not identity, meaning that a man cannot legally self-certify their way into women's changing rooms, toilets and sports.

None of this is complicated. Trans people deserve rights and equality and safety – but not at the expense of the rights and equality and safety of women. That means women get to keep separate spaces, separate medical services and separate sports. All of those things exist for the protection of women, who make up 50 per cent of the global population, as compared to the 0.1 per cent who have undertaken complex surgery to change their sex.

The rapid rise of the gender identity movement, which argued that sex is essentially irrelevant and that gender is merely a social construct, led to a kind of kamikaze empathy. Anybody who couldn't be persuaded that demolishing traditional gender norms was anything other than total insanity was dismissed for spouting right-wing bluster or smeared as 'transphobic'.

Some brave women have been punching back hard all along. The counter revolutionaries are led by adult human females like author J. K. Rowling, who has weathered vicious attacks on her character for speaking out but defiantly chose to barrel through them and stay true to her principles.

She is no great friend of mine. First, I have never seen a single minute of the *Harry Potter* movies nor read a word of the books. I'm aware that puts me in a very small and exclusive club of Potter cynics, but I prefer fast cars and explosions to broomsticks and potions. I'm very comfortable with that.

Secondly, she has whacked me repeatedly. We had a furious public spat a few years ago sparked by my friendship with Donald Trump (suffice it to say she is not a fan) during which she called me a 'fact-free, amoral, bigotry-apologizing celebrity toady'. She also publicly celebrated when a co-panellist on Bill Maher's *Real Time* told me to 'fuck off'.

Despite all of this, I've vocally defended Rowling for her views on women's rights in the face of hysterical abuse. And I think her dramatic defiance of the cancel culture mob is a revealing yardstick for exactly how far we have come.

Rowling is a survivor of horrific domestic abuse and sexual assault. She first told her story in a moving essay supporting a British campaigner who had outrageously been fired because she said – correctly – that 'sex is immutable and not to be conflated with gender identity'.

The young stars of the *Harry Potter* movies, including Daniel Radcliffe, Rupert Grint and Emma Watson, shamefully trashed Rowling as a bigot – planting their fangs squarely into the hand that has so generously fed their otherwise distinctly peckish careers.

Many more people around the world got to hear Rowling's personal story in *The Witch Trials of J. K. Rowling* podcast. She respectfully and incisively explained how she of all people understands the life-and-death importance of women being and feeling safe in women's spaces. The documentary was a chart-topping smash hit. It felt like a turning point. And if Rowling's resurgence is anything to go by, she is the one who's on the right side of history.

HBO commissioned a massive new *Harry Potter* TV show. Lucrative 'Harry Potter experiences' have sprung up at theme parks everywhere from London to LA and Riyadh. I obviously haven't checked with the hordes of people waiting in line – I'd rather paint over my TV and watch it dry – but none of them seem bothered that she's been cancelled for transphobia.

Similarly, when the video game *Hogwarts Legacy* – based on her *Harry Potter* franchise – was released, activists called for a boycott to stop Rowling 'profiting from her anti-trans views'. Instead it rocketed to the top as one of the fastest-selling games in history, raking in almost a billion dollars in a couple of weeks.

Remember that the whole campaign against Rowling began when she spoke up for a woman who was fired from her job at a think tank for tweeting, accurately, that transgender women cannot change their biological sex.

Rowling posted: 'Dress however you please. Call yourself whatever you like. Sleep with any consenting adult who'll have you. Live your best life in peace and security. *But force women out of their jobs for stating that sex is real?*'

I wish more people had the guts to follow their own common sense. Instead we've had years of performative hogwash and intelligence-insulting nonsense, which has been quietly alienating everybody who has a functioning brain.

Ketanji Brown Jackson is an Associate Justice of the Supreme Court of the United States, one of the most powerful legal roles on planet earth. She is the first black woman to ever hold that office – a fact that could have been celebrated for its symbolic empowerment.

Sadly President Biden, who picked her for the job, diminished that honour by gloating in advance that he would nominate '*a* black woman'. He could have waited to announce his pick and glorified her as the best-qualified legal scholar for the nation's top legal office, but Biden chose to imply the eventual nominee would be chosen because she happened to be a black woman.

At her confirmation hearing in the US Senate, Brown Jackson was asked outright by a female senator: 'Can you provide a definition for the word "woman"?' This is an entirely reasonable question. The US Supreme Court exists to uphold the constitution, protect civil rights and prevent discrimination, something of particular concern for the 170 million women who live there. If you're going to protect them, it stands to reason that you should know what they are.

'Can I provide a definition …?' began Brown Jackson's bonkers reply. 'I can't … Not in this context. I'm not a biologist.' What a load of smug, fatuous, grandstanding twaddle. I am not a vet but I have no problem telling the difference between a human and a horse. A year later Brown Jackson managed to rule in favour of the government's right to pressure social media companies over 'disinformation' – despite not being a computer scientist. How did she manage?

Defining a woman became a brain-melting riddle for some of the most important people in the world. Instead of simply saying what we all know to be true, they dance around the answer like prima ballerinas until they are painfully contorted into all kinds of back-breaking shapes.

Nicola Sturgeon was at one stage the most powerful female politician in the UK as leader of the separatist Scottish National Party. Asked by *The Times* newspaper to define a woman, she snapped: 'I'm not going to, I'm just not going to get into this debate at a level that's about simplified and lurid headlines.' It's not a debate, it's just a word – woman! You are one Nicola – and that's OK!

British Labour MP Sarah Owen appeared on BBC *Woman's Hour* – a woman-fronted show that's made for women and dedicated entirely to women's issues – shortly after being appointed Chair of the Women and Equalities Committee. Surely she of all people knows what a woman is? My jaw hit the floor as I listened to her answer the question – and by the time she had finished it had gone through the basement and was tunnelling rapidly towards the molten core of the earth.

Interviewer: 'Some of our listeners in particular would like to know – what is a woman to you?'

Owen: 'I think it's really sad that we're still at this stage of the debate, to be honest. And that we have boiled down people's fears or concerns on both sides of the argument to body parts – because basically we are so much more than what our bodies are. And what a woman to me is ... is somebody that is going to be paid less than their male counterpart. Somebody that is going to be less safe walking down the street ... And when it comes to the trans debate, we need to be able to have that in a kind, respectful way.... So, my committee will be made up of people that have different views and particularly on this topic and it will be my job to make sure that we find a way through ... But we need to see progress. And that progress starts with respect, understanding, and people being given a safe space to air their views.'

Wrong answer. Adult human female. Next question! Sir Keir Starmer, now the UK's Prime Minister (and Owen's boss), has had a 'woman' problem for years. His answer to the million-dollar question was to waffle that 'a woman is a female adult, and in addition to that, trans women are women, and that is not just my view'.

In a toe-curling radio interview he infamously asserted that 99.9 per cent of women 'haven't got a penis' (the correct stat is 100 per cent) and had previously condemned a female member of his own party for saying that only women have a cervix. Sir Ed Davey, leader of the Liberal Democrats, waded in to declare that women 'quite clearly' can have a penis. In 2022, the *Sun* newspaper ran the headline: 'Labour MPs at war again over whether a woman can be born with a penis'. Pause for a moment to imagine you have travelled to the present day in a time machine from 50 years ago. Now read this paragraph again. Just what the hell was going on?

Starmer won the UK election comfortably. But not before a screeching 180-degree turn that began with 'clearing up' his definition of a woman as 'an adult human female' in a BBC interview. He later declared that women's private spaces should be for women only. A poll had discovered a whopping 48 per cent of his own left-wing voters backed the Conservative position on single-sex services and only 20 per cent of his voters opposed it.

Only when the UK's Supreme Court made its landmark ruling this year did Starmer say with total confidence that men can't become women. 'I think it's very important that we've now got real clarity, which is going to be really helpful for, I think, everybody going forward,' he said. It may be helpful for you, going forward, Prime Minister. Most people have had real clarity on the matter since the beginning of human civilisation.

The same thing, of course, played out in the US election. Democrats failed to stand up to the activist fringe and liberal pundits scoffed that gender wasn't a 'kitchen table issue' – they said voters didn't really care. Clearly, they forgot to ask the voters! It was their repeated refusal to engage with very real concerns, dismissing them as bigotry and bluster, which made it a kitchen table issue. And they're still struggling to learn their lesson.

Hopeless governor Tim Walz was picked to run as Kamala Harris' vice-presidential nominee, apparently to improve Democrats' performance with white working-class men. Suffice it to say, the men weren't impressed. And on recent evidence, I don't suppose he's rating much better with women either. Congresswoman Nancy Mace asked him in 2025 if he could explain what a woman is at a congressional hearing. After an awkward pause, he replied: 'I'm not sure I understand the question here.'

At the very peak of the woke bubble – just as it was inflating to bursting point – I interviewed US singer Macy Gray on *Uncensored*. It was a wide-ranging interview with a charming, soulful popstar who has a lot of thoughtful things to say about the world.

Clearly, I had to ask her the burning question of the moment. 'A human being with boobs, I'll start there, and a vagina,' came the reply. 'Just because you go change your parts, doesn't make you a woman, sorry!' That was clearly her honestly held opinion and one that most women I know in real life would agree with. But I warned her she'd face a backlash. And so she did. The retribution was as vile as it was predictable. She was bombarded with torrents of abuse online and then branded an ignorant bigot and a transphobe.

Rolling Stone, the renegade magazine turned woke click-bait factory, wrote: 'One thing's for sure: Gray's antiquated, misguided, and hateful rhetoric surrounding trans people is the type of sentiment that has had deadly consequences.' Oh, come off it. Deadly consequences? For saying women have BOOBS? We learn that part of the anatomy as toddlers, just before we learn about the boy who cried wolf. Trans lobbyists have been wailing it at the top of their lungs for years now and we are no longer listening.

J. K. Rowling was one of the few celebrities to speak up for Macy, posting online: 'Today feels like a good day to ensure I've bought @MacyGraysLife's entire back catalogue.' It's not the first or the last time she has stuck her head above the parapet – knowing full well she'd face a storm force deluge from the Be Kind community.

A couple of days later Rowling followed up with a post responding to critics who said that she and other women's rights campaigners were incapable of handling 'mean comments'. She again hit the nail on the head: 'Endless death and rape threats, threats of loss of livelihood, employers targeted, physical harassment, family address posted online with picture of bomb-making manual aren't "mean comments". If you don't yet understand what happens to women who stand up on this issue, back off.'

WHAT *IS* A WOMAN?

Macy Gray, on the other hand, went on NBC's *Today* show to issue a humbling apology – no doubt under orders from her panicked publicists. This is why people don't stand up for women when it matters most. They get bullied and barracked until they submit to the vicious and vocal minority – even as the sane majority agrees with them. Ironically, these bullies are the same people who fought the US election on 'the threat to democracy'. It's not a democracy if your opinions are the only ones allowed.

Comedian and former sitcom star Roseanne Barr, who's had more cancellations than St Pancras Station, gets the final word on what a woman is. 'A woman is me,' she said in a chaotic interview on my show. 'A woman is somebody whose breasts hang down to her stomach, and who has a prolapsed uterus from giving birth to five ungrateful little bastards who have never had to work for a thing in their goddam life. *That's* what a woman is!' Roseanne was not invited by NBC to apologise, and I expect she'd have a blunt two-word answer if she was.

Not content with simply chewing it into mush, others have tried to dispose of the word 'woman' altogether. For some it has become a toxic word that must not be spoken. It may be alluded to – but never actually said.

Inconveniently, it refers to about 50 per cent of the world's population, which can make speaking quite difficult. Inclusive linguistic innovators have come up with many alternatives which are apparently less offensive: birthing people; menstruators; bodies with vaginas; individuals with a cervix; chestfeeders. These are all real examples of supposedly serious alternatives proposed by academics or deployed in health communications with the apparent aim of protecting trans people's feelings. My personal favourite is: 'Womxn'.

Wom-inx? Wom-exxon? Womex? How do you even say it? I have no idea. Former First Lady Michelle Obama used it on Instagram in a big post about abortion rights. One of the slides she shared said: 'State lawmakers will have the power to strip womxn of the right to make decisions about their bodies and their healthcare.' As I said on my show the next day – I am uncensored, so I can get away with some pretty shocking language – 'It's "woman", Michelle, and there is no "x" in woman.'

What made this so absurd is that Obama's post was supposed to be supporting women's rights. Instead, she trampled on them by pandering to a tiny minority of people who get upset when they hear a word that's been used for centuries to describe the people who aren't men.

The term 'womxn' is apparently a mark of respect to trans people who identify as women. But what about the mark of disrespect it shows the vast majority of women who just want to be called women? Where are their rights in all this virtue-signalling language-mangling? Reducing half of the world's population to an unpronounceable letter salad does nothing but deride women and draw mockery to the trans cause.

Cervical screening saves thousands of women's lives every year and could save thousands more if only more women knew about it. That's why governments and health officials around the world have made a huge effort in recent years to raise awareness and make it accessible to as many women as possible.

The Government of Jersey got in on the act with a social media campaign that said: 'If you are a transgender man, a gender non-conforming person, or assigned female at birth and with a cervix, you can book your free cervical screening today.'

The only word missing from its exhaustive list was the only one that needed to be on it – woman! A bearded man in a grey suit was the sole protagonist of the promotional photograph. Presumably he was an assigned-female-at-birth-and-with-a-cervix.

There's a serious reason why people get worked up about this and it was laid bare by the shocking case of Isla Bryson, which united the UK in disbelief. Bryson is the violent, convicted double rapist who later decided to self-identify as a woman and demand a place in an all-female prison.

Scottish First Minister Nicola Sturgeon publicly backed authorities when they allowed a convicted biologically male sex offender to move into an all-female facility, packed with potential new victims. Bryson's case spurred genuine fury about a separate Sturgeon-backed law allowing Scottish citizens to legally change their gender without needing a medical diagnosis of any kind. J. K. Rowling again led the charge, branding Sturgeon 'a destroyer of women's rights'.

A few days later she was gone. Sturgeon resigned as First Minister in disgrace. She was facing a slew of controversies at the time, but she had burned her political capital and shed many of her supporters over gender madness. One of the fiercest and most successful female leaders in the country sacrificed her career at the altar of identity politics.

Shortly after this repugnant charade I had an all-female panel on my show to mark International Women's Day. So far, so woke. But I spoiled the fun during a heated debate with an arch-liberal panellist who was attempting to justify limitless self-identity.

'Why can't I identify as a black lesbian?' I asked her. 'Why can't I say – I am Piers Morgan and I am a black lesbian?' She called me 'absurd'. My response was that the real absurdity is allowing anybody to put their hands in the air, declare womanhood and suddenly claim all of the rights and protections that women have. And what is more absurd than a strapping biological man, with all of the physical benefits of a male body, identifying as a woman and crushing biological women in their own sports? Eight million people watched the exchange on TikTok alone and the comments were rabidly in my favour. Suffice it to say that is not always the case. Clearly, I struck a nerve.

President Trump's declaration of gender common sense was an emphatic milestone at the end of a long and winding road back to normality. But he was as much a beneficiary of the backlash as its talisman. The fact he has twice denied America its first female president is a source of toe-stubbing agony for many feminists – partly because they know he's right about this.

The media narrative was that women would vote in historic droves for Kamala Harris on the sole basis that she is a woman. The election was often incorrectly cast as a 50–50 race that could only be determined by which candidate turned out more of their exclusively gendered base.

'The Gender Election', said the *New Yorker*. 'Men v Women', said the BBC. 'Why Gender May Be the Defining Issue of the Election', said the *New York Times*. But it wasn't. Women had plenty of reasons to vote overwhelmingly against Trump, not least on the issue of abortion rights and his long history of coarse statements about women, but they didn't.

Harris just about won more female voters overall but by a far smaller margin than all three of the previous Democrat candidates for president. A clear majority of white women backed Trump and he added seven points to his 2020 score with young women aged 18 to 29. How could this happen? Part of the answer, ironically given the abortion issue, is women's autonomy.

The Harris campaign bombarded women with patronising ads which cast them as defenceless little creatures needing protection from the big orange menace. Julia Roberts voiced an ad with the slogan: 'What happens in the booth, stays in the booth.' Two timid wives are shown entering a polling booth, where they sneak conspiratorial glances at one another before secretly voting for Kamala Harris.

The Oscar-winning actress declares: 'In the one place in America where women still have a right to choose, you can vote any way you want and no one will ever know.' Many female voters chose to back Trump because they wanted to – not because they are 1950s Stepford Wives living in fear of their crazed MAGA husbands.

I firmly believe that one of the reasons so many made that choice is that the other side threw their whole lot in with the woman-erasing fanatics and a candidate who publicly backed taxpayer-funded sex changes for illegal immigrants. It's extremely revealing that Rahm Emanuel, who wants to run as the next Democratic president, gave an interview in July 2025 in which he stated emphatically that men cannot become women.

Trans people are not the problem in all of this, as I've always said. Any adult who suffers genuine dysmorphia and goes through a multi-year ordeal and major surgery to transform their bodies has clearly put some thought into it. They should absolutely have the same rights to fairness and equality as anybody else, as well as our respect.

The problem is really the people who wage self-serving virtue wars on their behalf; pushing ridiculous extremes that end up eroding the rights of women. I don't give a damn about the identity chameleons at this point. Nobody cares any more. Singer Sam Smith, for example, has had about a hundred gender identities so far. I find the insatiable thirst for attention quite exhausting. But I did not lose any sleep when Smith announced a transition from 'genderqueer' to 'nonbinary' – quite the opposite, in fact!

In a free society you can choose to identify and label yourself as you please. The rest of us can choose not to participate in your delusions – or to support your rights up to the point they start curtailing the rights of everybody else. And last time I checked, Sam Smith isn't demanding unfettered access to women's bathrooms or the right to fight women competitively. Women's rights have been very hard-fought and we have to fight to defend them too. That begins with knowing and saying what they are.

Chapter 8

IT'S SPORT, BUT NOT AS WE KNOW IT

Trans women in female sports is cheating on steroids – or hormonal therapy.

'The war on women's sports is over,' President Trump declared as he banned transgender athletes from competing in US women's sports. He beckoned for the watching crowd of beaming schoolgirls to huddle close around his desk as he signed the order. 'I think I'm going to be OK,' Trump joked to the twitchy secret service agents. 'If we have to worry about them we have big problems.' The girls looked thrilled and so did he.

Trump has been smeared as a bigot, a misogynist, an abuser and worse. This wholesome, almost grandfatherly scene – one of the defining images of his second presidency so far – was a spectacular repudiation. And the contrast of these giggling schoolgirls beside the burly President could hardly have been more appropriate for the subject matter.

The pictures and the story made every news bulletin on planet earth. 'Congratulations to every single person on the left who's been campaigning to destroy women's and girls' rights,' wrote J. K. Rowling, adding: 'Without you, there'd be no images like this.' She's right. Woke fanatics gave him a free shot and he took it.

Tennis legend Martina Navratilova, who likes Trump as much as she likes toothache, shared the video with the comment: 'I hate that the Democrats totally failed women and girls on this very clear issue of women's sports being for females only.' Martina is a lifelong progressive who has donated large sums of money to the Democrats.

She also came out as a lesbian in the early 1980s – one of the first major athletes ever to do so – and has spent decades fighting for gay rights and feminism. It takes a common-sense chasm of Grand Canyon proportions for her to end up on the same side as Trump about anything.

Democrats had four years to seize the middle ground on this issue as it raged out of control. Instead Biden declared Easter Sunday to be 'Trans Day of Visibility' and invited trans activists to the White House, where three guests ended up being banned for posing topless in front of the presidential mansion, which was draped in Pride flags.

This is why most American voters looked at a perma-tanned billionaire realtor who lives in a gilded tower and decided *he* was the normal one. Find me a parent anywhere who wants their young daughter kicked on a sports pitch by a male – or wants their son to do the kicking. Find me a sports fan anywhere who wants to watch men obliterating women. It will be a long search.

The scandal of biological men in women's sports has never really been about trans rights. It's about what should always have been screamingly obvious. Fairness! Sport lives and dies on fairness. Athletes born with balls have irrefutable physical advantages over those born without them. They're stronger, have bigger bones, greater natural stamina, more muscle mass and bigger lungs for endurance. There is no amount of surgery that can change that.

Trans women in female sports is cheating on steroids – or hormonal therapy, anyway. And as with so much else in the woke obituary, the kid gloves are now off. Polite and reasoned objection was met with increasingly outrageous insults to common sense until eventually the whole farce was flattened by a clunking fist.

Sadly, that was also the fate of Italy's boxer Angela Carini at the Paris Olympics in 2024. She was almost literally knocked out of the competition by Algerian boxer Imane Khelif, a biological male, who went on to win the women's welterweight gold medal. If it walks like a duck, quacks like a duck and fights like a duck, it probably is a duck. Anyone who watched the sad spectacle of Khelif beating up Carini knew they were not really watching a woman.

So did Carini, which is why she quit the bout after 40 seconds and later wept in front of TV cameras as she revealed she'd never been hit so hard in her life and feared she'd be killed if she carried on. The crowd knew it too because they booed. And the International Boxing Association knew it, because they banned Khelif from competing in the Women's World Championships for failing tests to meet the 'eligibility criteria' for participating in women's competition.

Khelif has a rare disorder that can lead to sufferers incorrectly thinking they are female until they reach adulthood. There may have been confusion over Khelif's sex, and Khelif may have genuinely identified as a biological female. But the facts say otherwise. This was clarified by a medical report a full year before the Olympics and the IOC knew it. So why did it still let Khelif compete against, and beat – in every sense – other women?

The answer is moral cowardice. The IOC was terrified of blowback from the woke mob, which mobilises viciously against anyone who dares stand up to this nonsense. It hasn't submitted athletes to chromosomal testing for years and its only requirement for participation at the Paris Olympics in women's boxing was to have a female sex marker on legal documents. In other words, you just say you're a woman on a form and bingo, you're fighting against women – even if, like Khelif, you're biologically a man.

The Olympics are supposed to be the pinnacle of athletic probity; civilisation's ultimate test of sporting prowess in a global arena where only talent and discipline can win the ultimate battle of wills. Female paralympic sprinters lining up for the 400-metre semi-final, just weeks after the Khelif travesty, instead faced a battle of the bulge.

Italian runner Valentina Petrillo ran alongside them, despite being 51 years old and sporting a strikingly visible penis-shaped protrusion. Petrillo, who won a dozen sprint titles as a man before transitioning at age 45, said competing in Paris was the fulfilment of a 'dream since I was a little girl'. But by competing in the games, Petrillo stole another actual woman's dream of sport's top honour – one who, unlike Petrillo, really was a little girl once. It was a fitting end to a summer Games whose opening ceremony bizarrely celebrated 'queer love' and recreated the Last Supper with drag queens.

Former US college swimmer Lia Thomas is the flag-bearer for trans athletes and may unwittingly have become the catalyst for the end of the farce. Thomas was a mediocre performer when competing as a man but became a record-breaking phenomenon as a woman – winning some races by several whole laps of the pool.

Thomas made history in 2022, becoming the first transgender woman to win an NCAA championship. That is the top prize in college sports, which are hugely popular in the US and a conveyor belt to professional sporting stardom. ESPN preposterously featured Thomas in a special show to mark Women's History Month.

Podium pictures show Thomas towering over biologically female competitors; male appendages on full display. Authorities could have intervened at many different waypoints on the swimmer's ascent to the top but they didn't. Instead it snowballed into a global soap opera, which made both Thomas and competitive swimming the object of ridicule. A demonstrably scandalous situation was allowed to continue unchecked because most people were too scared of cancellation to put their heads over the parapet and demand an end to the circus.

Thomas added insult to injury by appearing on a podcast to trash women, accusing female critics of 'using the guise of feminism to ... push transphobic beliefs'.

Martina Navratilova said it best, replying simply: 'Stop explaining feminism to feminists.'

Feminism is the fight for equality of the sexes, male and female. Many newly equal rights have been hard-fought over many decades, including the right to compete in professional sports at all and the simple right to privacy and safety from harassment by men. Now someone born a man can choose to enter those female sports, demolish all the women and demand the right to be in the room where they get undressed.

And this is a totally one-way violation because women who identify as men have no such potency in male sports – nor will they be remotely intimidating in the locker room. No wonder feminists are hopping mad. As for the ubiquitous 'transphobia' barb – a phobia is an irrational fear. But I'd say it is completely rational for a woman to feel uneasy when a 6-ft figure with a penis is roaming around a room of naked women. If I was Lia Thomas, and we're not so very unalike, I'd sit out the feminism debate.

At the peak of Thomas' infamy I interviewed Caitlyn Jenner on *Uncensored*. Caitlyn is probably better qualified to comment on this than anybody, having smashed a world record to win Olympic gold as male decathlete Bruce Jenner.

'Lia Thomas is one of the worst things that happened to the trans community because it's such bad publicity,' she told me. Thomas' notoriety pitched trans people against women in an unwinnable war of common sense – even though most trans women did not want the battle.

Jenner even refuses to play in all-women's golf tourna-ments because of her inexorable physical advantages, explaining: 'I have no more testosterone going through my body, and I can still outdrive all the girls by 100 yards. I can reach every par five in two. It's just not fair.' And that, right there, is the crux of the matter.

Jenner herself has been repeatedly and ludicrously branded a 'transphobe' despite being, well, trans. That is the inevitable and farcical end point for a merciless movement that demands total uncompromising fealty to its impossibly narrow worldview.

Former college swimmer Riley Gaines, who I've interviewed many times, has found that out the hard way. She had vowed to win the NCAA title in 2022. But that was the same year that the NCAA allowed Thomas, previously ranked 554th as a man, to dive into the female competition. The world knows what happened next.

Gaines has since made it her mission to campaign for women's rights in sport; touring college campuses to share her story. For that she has received a barrage of death threats and endless harassment. She even found herself barricaded into a side room at San Francisco State University while angry protesters banged on the door shouting 'we want Riley' and 'don't protect a transphobe'.

Shortly after the story broke, I appeared on Bill Maher's HBO show alongside Democrat Congresswoman Katie Porter. She accused Gaines of exploiting the incident for 'likes and clicks', adding pointedly that 'Riley is speaking up for *herself* and I respect her prerogative'. At that point I butted in to say: 'I think she's speaking up for pretty much *every* female athlete in the world.'

Maher's famously woke audience burst into applause – for me! A crowd of Democrats, smack bang in the middle of true-blue Los Angeles, rooting for Piers Morgan against a progressive female Democrat politician? I knew right then that the woke worm was turning.

Teenage runner Aayden Gallagher became the Oregon girls' 200-metre state champion in May 2024, posting one of the fastest times in the state's history with a remarkable display of power and stamina. But as Aayden crossed the finish line, something startling happened. Instead of joyous cheering and adulation, the watching crowd started angrily booing her.

The same thing happened when Gallagher received a gold medal on the podium – even as the runner-up was loudly cheered for her silver. There was a very simple explanation for this and there is no gold medal for guessing it.

Gallagher is a transgender athlete who was born a male, with a vastly superior physiology to show for it. As viral video clips from the race show, Gallagher towered over many of the competing girls, displaying vastly greater height, power and speed that made a mockery of any pretence of fairness.

The reaction of this modest high school crowd is a small moment in the grand scheme of things, but it was more evidence of a dramatic shift in social attitudes. A few years ago this would have been a completely different story. The crowd would have stood in ovation. Gallagher's win would have been hailed as the latest symbolic victory for progressive inclusivity and tolerance. But we're no longer buying what they're selling. Tolerance and inclusivity can't exclude women's rights and be intolerant for women.

The Oregon School Activities Association, which governs high school sports, say they allow students to participate in the athletic or activity programme of their 'consistently asserted' gender identity. Really? That is pandering buffoonery which can only possibly be explained by the fear of being branded a bigot.

It's exactly the type of bureaucratic do-gooding that sounds oh-so-virtuous in boardroom meetings but trickles down as horrendous injustices in real life. Anybody who has raised – or in fact been – a teenager should be fully aware that consistent assertions are an irritation that should be consistently averted. If a student consistently asserts dominion of a classroom by identifying as a teacher, they will be booted out of the school.

A flimsy self-certification, in the middle of a huge social contagion, does not justify sacrificing the enjoyment and safety of girls whose gender is asserted by their actual chromosomes. You can demand that trans people's choices are respected and their rights to fairness and equality are protected. I will demand that with you. But you can't 'assert' rights at the cost of women's rights to fairness and equality in their own sport. For years, that view has been shamed and vilified as heretic. The reaction of that crowd in Oregon showed that the silenced majority was now fighting back – and it soon started to get results.

Sporting bodies around the world have all finally started banning transgender athletes from women's sports. World Rugby became the first in 2020 – banning trans women from competing in elite competitions including the Olympics and Rugby World Cup. 'Safety and fairness cannot presently be assured for women competing against trans women,' the authority said in its new guidance, noting that at least one injury typically occurs in every rugby match.

Athlete Ally, an LGBTQIA+ sports advocacy group, led the thunderous complaints by arguing that there is no recorded evidence of transgender women causing serious injuries to 'cisgender women' (aka women). But that is precisely the point. World Rugby stepped in before the inevitable happened. Why wait until a woman is badly hurt, or for the chilling spectacle of the Olympic boxing, before doing the right thing?

World Aquatics, the international governing body for swimming, was the next domino to fall. It banned transgender women from competing in major international female swimming competitions if they have already been through male puberty. That meant Lia Thomas, who was farcically the top young women's swimmer in America heading into the Paris Olympics, was barred from taking part in the qualifiers.

Thomas fought a legal battle to overturn the decision at the Court of Arbitration for Sport in Switzerland, citing discrimination, but the appeal was rejected. Athlete Ally called it 'a sad day for sports' and Thomas said the verdict was 'a call to action to all trans women athletes to continue to fight for our dignity and human rights'. There is obviously no human right to compete as a woman at the Olympics – not at the expense of the dignity of women who have invested their whole lives in doing exactly that. And especially not if you are a man.

World Athletics chief Lord Sebastian Coe was next to announce a total ban on post-puberty trans athletes in female international events. Lord Coe said the decision had been taken to 'protect the future of the female category' and that it was their duty to 'maintain fairness for female athletes above all other considerations'. Hallelujah.

He also said the authority would be 'guided by the science' on male physical advantage and by using those words he acknowledged the simple truth underpinning this whole debate: biological sex is an irrefutable scientific fact. It's ironic that 'trust the science' became a woke mantra during the Covid pandemic, but the same people are selectively deaf to 'the science' when it comes to women being walloped by men in sports.

Covid taught many people a lesson about healthy inquisitive scepticism, me included, not least because science is ever-evolving and necessarily mistrusting of itself. But it underlines the back-breaking logical gymnastics of woke ideology. Science is gospel on masks, vaccines and climate change but irrelevant or wrong on sex and gender because it does not fit the woke script.

That's not how it works! Why did it take a man to say it?

There is no need whatsoever for this kind of common sense to be 'right-wing' or even conservative. The great American anti-slavery author Harriet Beecher Stowe said: 'Common sense is seeing things as they are; and doing things as they ought to be.' That is really all this boils down to.

None of the sporting bodies that are now finally banning trans athletes are remotely right-wing. They did not make these decisions because of protests by people like Martina Navratilova, J. K. Rowling or indeed me – and none of us are right-wing either. The political left, especially in America, allowed itself to be captured and directed by fanatics at the extreme margins.

Take the case of Democrat Congressman Seth Moulton, who waded into the issue of trans athletes shortly before the US election by writing: 'I have two little girls. I don't want them getting run over on a playing field by a formerly male athlete, but as a Democrat I'm supposed to be afraid to say that.' What happened next shows exactly why he was supposed to be afraid. His own party fired up the full machinery of the cancellation playbook.

Moulton's local selection committee said it would find a challenger to unseat him in the next primary; a department chief at the state university said it would cancel internships for his staff and a prominent city councillor demanded his immediate resignation. Steve Kerrigan, chairman of the Democratic Party in Massachusetts, said the comments 'do not represent the broad view of our Party'. Moulton's own campaign manager then quit in fury.

Moulton had expressed an honestly held view that any sane voter would agree with and was met with a fascist-worthy crushing of his apparent dissent. I can't think of a better example of why the Democrats were humiliated in the US election. They should listen more to Seth Moulton and less to the squealing campaign manager who ended his own career to protect penises in women's locker rooms.

The tide has now turned on this madness but, as with so many of these stories, it leaves many victims already washed up on the shore. A UN report on 'violence against women and girls in sports' revealed that more than 600 female athletes in various competitions in 29 different sports have lost more than 890 medals because of athletes born as men.

There was a sign-of-the-times silliness in pictures of strapping trans women, bulges intact, showing up to race women. But it gets a lot less funny when you remember the embarrassment and disappointment of the women whose dreams were shattered and privacy violated.

'I don't want to see a naked man's genitalia,' Riley Gaines said in a heated debate on *Uncensored*. 'I'm married. Do you think my husband wants me seeing another naked man while he also gets to simultaneously, non-consensually, see me naked? No way. That goes against my values.' She was inevitably accused by another guest of discrimination, to which she snapped back: 'It's discriminating against *us* on the basis of *our* sex.' How can anybody honestly say she is wrong?

All of this has been bizarrely cheered on by a complicit media that felt it was duty-bound to normalise obvious insanity. Of the 40,000 athletes who ran the 2023 London Marathon, the BBC decided to interview Glenique Frank, a 54-year-old transgender woman who – unsurprisingly –

placed ahead of 14,000 female runners. The UK's top TV channel had considerably less airtime available when Frank apologised, offered to forfeit the medal and vowed to voluntarily run in the male category in future.

The news headlines were just as lopsided after President Trump signed the executive order. NPR warned of 'extremism' with 'echoes in history', while the *New York Times* lamented 'Trump's Shameful Campaign Against Transgender Americans' and *USA Today* moaned that 'the pomp and circumstance didn't hide the ugliness of the moment'. Polls have repeatedly shown that most voters back a ban on trans women in women's sports – and they had just emphatically elected the man who was doing it after promising that he would do it. So why was the coverage so funereal?

CeCé Telfer, an unremarkable male college runner who became a record-setting woman after transitioning, got top billing on CNN for an interview bemoaning the 'unfairness' of the policy. 'Now I wake up every day and I have to make sure that I make it home alive,' she said. So do I, CeCé, but smashing women's sporting records is not part of my survival plan. And what about 'fairness' for the women you embarrass on the track?

I posted my disdain on X and immediately received a backlash – from conservatives! 'Absurd CNN interview,' I wrote, 'she was born male, looks & speaks like a man, runs like a man, and is smashing women's records. She's not a victim, she's a cheat.'

Hordes of prominent commentators, led by none other than Riley Gaines, chastised me for calling CeCé a 'she'.

But that's just a matter of politeness in my eyes. I don't have an issue with transgender people calling themselves 'she', or requesting that other people do the same, as long as it's my choice and not a legally-binding command. Trans people do exist and they should exist in their own trans category in elite sports – or compete as their birth-determined sex. Identity is complicated and personal, but biology is just fact.

Many liberals who appear on *Uncensored* argue there are so few trans athletes that it's just not worth the government's time or the media's coverage. I vehemently disagree. Even one outrageous case like that of Lia Thomas is one too many – it says a lot about the chaos and degradation in politics that for so long nothing was done to stop it. And even if I go by their logic, what can possibly justify the global hysteria about banning it if it's really such a tiny and piddling minority concern?

President Trump simply read the room and filled a common-sense void; winning begrudging approval from some of his fiercest critics. Just 24 hours after his executive action the NCAA, which governs all US college sports and shamefully enabled the whole Lia Thomas scandal, reversed a 15-year policy and banned transgender women. Thomas has now been stripped of all the titles and records. And in July 2025 the US Olympic Committee banned transgender athletes from representing the USA in women's categories.

When feted US Olympic gymnast Simone Biles recently decided to attack Riley Gaines as a sick bully for opposing trans athletes in women's sport, she no doubt expected to have the weight of public opinion behind her. Instead it was Biles who was forced to issue an apology and deactivate her account because of the backlash. How times have changed!

Riley Gaines missed out on a chance at sporting glory because of the NCAA and Lia Thomas. The whole world saw the picture of her standing behind Thomas at the podium – looking exhausted, demoralised and confused. Look a bit closer at that iconic image of Trump and the schoolgirls in the White House and you will spot a smiling, smartly dressed figure standing proudly behind him to witness the moment of history. It was Riley Gaines. Sometimes winning is a marathon, not a sprint.

PART THREE
UNCENSORED

No stones were left unturned in the relentless quest
to remodel our wicked world as a woke utopia.
From ludicrous word bans and a whole new
dictionary to tediously moralising movies,
hypocritical preaching celebrities, TV commercials
that shamed us all as nasty bigots and a maniacal
campaign to 'save the planet' by throwing soup
around in art galleries and forcing everybody to eat
vegan gruel. It's been exhausting. But each and every
one of the following chapters is a heartening fable of
radical overreach and triumphant popular
resistance. Woke broke it. We fixed it!

Chapter 9

GO WOKE, GO BROKE

I don't need a rainbow on my breakfast cereal,
sandwich or chocolate bar to prove that I don't care
what you get up to in your spare time.

The Super Bowl is corporate Christmas for the US. Everybody celebrates – whether they believe in American Football or not. Tens of millions get together to drink beer and eat garbage as they indulge in a riotous afternoon of celeb-spotting, extravagant half-time entertainment and lavish star-studded commercials, which get as much coverage as the game. There is a sports final in there somewhere, too. But in recent years the Super Bowl has become a pulpit for corporate America to pontificate about social justice and browbeat viewers for their wickedness.

Beyoncé performed with dancers dressed as Black Panthers; a crew of all-female pilots was assembled for a military flyover; ads weighed in on hot-button politics like illegal immigration (and, criminally, featured men with papooses). Players even charged towards endzones emblazoned with the words 'END RACISM' in giant letters, lest anyone think the football game itself might be a break from the endless moralising and dour realities of everyday life. President Trump waged a verbal war on the NFL during his first term over players' performative knee-taking for racial justice during the national anthem; a practice that turned sporting escapism into a massive divisive mess. Ratings began to ebb.

Super Bowl LIX felt like a time capsule from a bygone age of entertainment innocence. The 'END RACISM' lettering was axed. Trump himself showed up – the first-ever sitting president to do so – and his favourite patriotic anthem, 'God Bless the USA', blared out across the stadium. Kendrick Lamar's half-time show was unmemorable musically but notable for its substitution of Marxist revolutionaries for backing dancers in red, white and blue who huddled to form a big American flag.

Patriotism was back in place of politics and everything felt reassuringly *normal*. Trump's mere presence was a spectacular thawing of frozen relations. Some of the NFL's top stars, backed by their commissioner Roger Goodell, traded vicious blows with the president over Black Lives Matter protests in 2020. Yet here he was, shaking hands with Goodell and getting a rapturous ovation from the crowd, at the end of a season in which his YMCA dad dance became a wildly popular on-field celebration among players. The message was that sport and the Super Bowl is for everyone again – black, white, MAGA red, liberal blue – as it should be.

Evidence of a volcanic shift was most glaring in the Super Bowl ads, which are a powerful cultural barometer in a capitalism-crazed culture where people unashamedly love brands and love buying stuff. Pringles celebrated men with moustaches; Stella Artois paired Matt Damon and David Beckham for a beer-and-wings bro-fest; Nike's ad was a worthy girl power affair but it notably vaunted a load of actual women who play actual women's sports against other actual women. Two years earlier it used a boobless trans woman to model its sports bras.

Fast-food chain Carl's Jr. came out swinging, too. At the 2015 Super Bowl it was accused of 'setting feminism back decades' by using a bikini-clad model munching on a giant juicy burger. The company later grovelled with a new marketing strategy focused on 'food, not boobs'. But this year, the boobs were back!

A bikini-clad blonde influencer flaunted a 'free hangover burger' before speeding off down the street in a gas-guzzling vintage sports car. And honestly, why not? I have never understood the feminist case against bikinis. Women who look good in bikinis generally enjoy wearing them, and men are entitled to quietly and tastefully enjoy them doing so. The entire human race depends on that dynamic. And if the purpose of the ad was to promote 'hangover burgers' to millions of hungover men, I'd say mission accomplished.

Most remarkable of all was the big budget Super Bowl campaign by Bud Light, whose journey down the virtue-signalling rabbit hole and back again is a microcosm of the entire death of woke. Bud Light was America's best-selling beer for decades and a beloved brand for millions of easygoing, sports-loving American men.

Any Brit will tell you that it is not really beer at all – but that did not stop them shifting 400 million cases of the stuff every year. For 22 years in the top spot Bud Light swatted away fashionable low-calorie rivals, repelled an invasion of Latino challengers and bravely fought the rise of trendy craft beers with their ghastly fruit flavourings and multicolour cans. The world was changing but Bud Light would remain the same. Smart and funny ad campaigns, all based on regular guys making fun of regular guy problems, cemented its place as the US beer king. But then along came Dylan Mulvaney.

On 1 April 2023, Bud Light launched a massive social media marketing campaign with the transgender activist and TikTok star, whose whole shtick is a saccharine performance of grossly exaggerated female stereotypes. In the video Mulvaney jokes about struggling to carry the beers, coos about not understanding sports and then raises a can of Bud Light to toast her '365 days of womanhood'. The company even made a can with Mulvaney's face on it to mark this momentous anniversary.

This may go down as the biggest corporate branding blunder in history. The second biggest was not pretending it was all an April Fool's joke. Sales plunged 26 per cent in just weeks. By mid-2023, Bud's owner Anheuser-Busch InBev had lost over $15 billion in market value and laid off hundreds of workers.

The beer's loyal, mostly male customers took it as a socking great punch in the balls, ironically. Conservatives were the public face of the Bud boycott – MAGA musician Kid Rock opened fire on a case with a semi-automatic rifle – but Bud Light managed to piss off just about everybody. Data showed millions of people were offended, liberals included, and even the LGBT activists complained about exploitative tokenism.

Bud Light's new Super Bowl LIX ad was a whiplash-inducing 180-degree turn and a man-tastic, knees-bent, palms-clenched plea for forgiveness. Titled 'Big Men on Cul-De-Sac', the one-minute bro comedy stars anti-woke comedian Shane Gillis, rapper Post Malone and (Republican-voting) NFL legend Peyton Manning. They throw an impromptu summer barbecue party for the guys on their all-American picket-fenced street, shooting cold blue cans of Bud Light from leaf blowers while Huey Lewis and the News blares in the background. It's one breath short of shouting 'MEN, WE LOVE YOU!'

Kid Rock is now back onside with Bud Light after crisis talks with the Anheuser-Busch CEO. And the company has ploughed $100 million into sponsoring Dana White's Ultimate Fighting Championship, a free speech-lauding macho combat sports franchise that is mutually revered by Donald Trump. It's the most excruciating public apology since Bill Clinton's sexual relations with 'that woman'. But sales remain 40 per cent down on pre-Mulvaney levels. It is no longer number one and may never be again. Millions of Americans simply did not want their beer to be pro-trans, anti-trans, or really any trans. They just wanted a beer.

No one company has sacrificed more dollars at the woke altar, but the Bud Light backlash was powered by pent-up fury about a whole gluttonous array of hectoring advertisers. Corporate marketeers blazed through red light after red light until they eventually smashed into a wall of customer resistance.

Big social issues and moral panics inevitably come and go. They're divisive in the first place and our collective views about them tend to change over time, which only makes it more ridiculous that brands – the best of which are consistent and reliable across many generations – started weighing in on them.

The original cautionary tale is of course Gillette, which became one of the world's biggest shaving brands with its masculinity-hailing tagline 'the best a man can get'. For years its glossy adverts showcased good-looking, hard-working men who were great at sports and dedicated to their families.

Think young dads kissing their babies while knotting their ties for work; beaming fathers embracing tuxedo-clad sons beside a wedding chapel; traders clenching their fists in celebration in a bustling stock exchange. All inter-spersed with hero shots of sporting champions giving their all to *win*. Fine, that's not the reality for most men. But what is wrong with aspiring for it to be that little bit closer to reality? Absolutely nothing!

Instead of embracing their winning message of 30 years' standing, Gillette rode the coat-tails of the MeToo movement with a now-infamous sermon of an ad that asked: 'Is *this* the best a man can get?' Young men were depicted as toxic, bullying, cat-calling, arse-grabbing, woman-patronising beasts who need to save one another from their own inevitable genetic depravity. Unsurprisingly, men hated it and the company lost billions. Its newest advert showcases proud fathers, doting sons, supportive friends and a whole lot of winning.

Advertising is supposed to shove products down our throats. Everybody knows that. At their best, ads make us smile, laugh, even cry. They make us associate brands with feelings so that we choose to buy their products. That is the deal and it has been for generations. But woke era marketing transformed the whole process into a lecture.

The advertisers' job is to read the room, but instead they stood on a soapbox in the middle of that room and yelled at everyone in it for being racist. Every billboard, magazine page and TV spot became an opportunity to tell us how to be a better person. Boardrooms rose up as one and decided it was their duty to not only sell you toilet paper and T-shirts but a greater moral purpose.

Calvin Klein celebrated Mother's Day with a pregnant man. Make-up merchant Maybelline sloshed shiny pink lipstick on a big, bearded bloke with a bald head. Shaving firm Braun used to sell its razors on max power, optimal performance and precision engineering – everything I see in the mirror – but switched to using a trans model with visible scars.

These companies have either monumentally mistaken their own hyper-liberal worldviews for the public mood – or this was always industrial scale gaslighting. Either way, more often than not they turn out to be stinking hypocrites because they never live up to the standards they set for everybody else.

I'm going to tell you a story now. It's about a marketing campaign so hopelessly absurd that I am convinced it was designed – specifically – to irritate me. Not long ago, in a faraway Kingdom (United), HSBC commissioned a children's author to rewrite three classic fairytales for a new book. You might well think that's an unusual thing for a bank to do, so – if you're sitting comfortably – I'll allow them to explain.

'[The] new book challenges traditional gender stereotypes,' the press release said, acknowledging that financial attitudes can be shaped as early as five years old. The book – *Fairer Tales: Princesses Doing It for Themselves* – re-imagines Cinderella, Sleeping Beauty and Rapunzel as successful businesswomen. Prince Charming is inevitably erased as the main character. And because this is a bank, and banks have lots of money, they hired tennis star Emma Raducanu to awkwardly read the stories aloud in a series of toe-curling videos.

Apologies for spoiling the ending, but Raducanu signs off with: 'So in the end, the princesses didn't need a prince to save them. They set up their own businesses, saved their money and then spent it very wisely.'

Of course, the best way to raise the aspirations of women is by abolishing men. And as Emma says, women don't need men at all. She has never needed any men, besides her father – who manages her career and, well, fathered her. Plus her eight male coaches. Or her agent, who is clearly very good at maximising her earnings potential, despite being a man.

Obesity-peddling ice cream brand Ben & Jerry's goes out of its way to insult customers – and at the most tone-deaf moments. The Fourth of July is a special day for Americans (and a sore one for Brits): a day for friends and family to celebrate freedom with parades, fireworks, recitals of the Declaration of Independence beside roaring bonfires, and lots of jokes about running the redcoats out of town.

Ben & Jerry's chose this unifying occasion to post: 'The US was founded on stolen Indigenous land. This year, let's commit to returning it.' The company demanded Mount Rushmore be handed over to Native Americans and trashed presidents Washington, Jefferson, Lincoln and Theodore Roosevelt as villains who 'actively worked to destroy Indigenous cultures and ways of life, to deny Indigenous people their basic rights'.

Right below was a cynical plea for viewers to sign up for its mailing list for the 'inside scoop' on new flavours. Many social media users quickly pointed out that its headquarters in Vermont is built on land 'stolen' from the native Abenaki tribe, which quickly demanded reparations. B&J co-founder Ben Cohen was then found to have donated $1 million to a group lobbying to end US aid for Ukraine, whose land has been stolen by Russia. It ain't easy being a wokey.

As well as campaigning to give away the United States, Ben & Jerry's says it is 'never going to stop trying … to end the climate crisis and fight for our democracy'. Its parent company Unilever has done copious amounts of business with famously democracy-loving Russia and China, who happen to be global chart-toppers for apparently climate-wrecking pollution.

Unilever has also been whacked by Greenpeace for 'poisoning our planet' with rampant plastic waste. It's a textbook case of ripping off gullible wokesters who think buying the right ice cream can somehow save the world – and infuriating the landslide majority who just want to buy ice cream.

Big oil and gas companies play this fake green card with impunity. Luscious forests, windmills and solar panels festoon their ads, with 100 per cent of the marketing budget spent on flaunting impossible 'net-zero' plans that make up a microscopic spec of their fuel-burning billions.

Oil and gas giant BP, responsible for the Deepwater Horizon disaster and one of the biggest polluters in history, popularised the whole concept of a 'carbon footprint'. Sensitive customers guiltily add up the number of polar bears they've slain buying BP's products, while the company carries on pumping oil and gas, developing new fields and profiting handsomely. Judging by the number of blue-haired protesters they attract, this pandering was again rejected by the very people it was supposed to appease.

The month of Pride is the dizzying peak of hypocritical corporate virtue-signalling. Pride began in the 1970s as a laudable day of protests and marches for gay rights. The very first Pride day marked the anniversary of the Stonewall riots, where gay people fought back against systematic harassment by police.

Homosexuality was illegal then and gays were routinely subjected to shocking abuse and vicious discrimination. That is thankfully no longer the case. But the only thing that has expanded faster than gay rights is the movement demanding them. L and G met B and T before eventually joining Q, I and A and then 2SL+. The rainbow Pride flag has morphed into a migrainous kaleidoscopic nightmare that is plastered onto every conceivable product and billboard for an entire calendar month.

I don't need a rainbow on my breakfast cereal, sandwich or chocolate bar to prove that I don't care what you get up to in your spare time. And it turns out that many gay people agree.

Burger King presented a Pride whopper, which came with either two 'top' buns or two 'bottom' buns. Gay people quickly pointed out that this fundamentally misunderstands how the system works. The company apologised for offending the LGBT community (but not for spoiling lunch for everybody else).

Posh supermarket Marks & Spencer had a gay BLT sandwich. The LGBT paired lettuce, guacamole, bacon and tomato. It left a foul taste on multiple levels. Activists were unhappy with being reduced to sandwich form and derided the company's claim that it had donated £10,000 to charity.

Rainbow-coloured candy Skittles confusingly released an all-white edition, which totally erased their usual accidental use of the Pride flag. And conservatives were outraged by packaging that ludicrously included the words 'black trans lives matter' on a product aimed at children.

The US Marine Corps even got in on the act by posting a 'Proud to Serve' poster featuring a camo helmet and a load of bullets in the colours of the Pride flag. Openly gay people were banned from the US military until 2011 and it's fair to say that very few Pride marchers are keen on being represented by deadly munitions.

Car-maker BMW changed its logo for a rainbow version across social media for Pride 2024. This is a now-ubiquitous act of corporate solidarity. But followers in the Middle East, where homosexuality is commemorated rather differently, got the plain old blue and white. After a backlash, the company explained: 'This is an established practice at the BMW Group, which also takes into consideration market-specific legal regulations and country-specific cultural aspects.'

In other words, we will bravely champion gay rights but only in the places where nobody actually needs us to. And that is really the point here. Brands don't care about gay rights. They're not making a stand. They are adjusting their messaging to amplify their virtue so they can sell you their products. And as the very unhappy marriage of Dylan Mulvaney and Bud Light shows, they will drop the cause like a flaming hot potato when it starts costing them money.

US department store Target followed this same well-trodden path from rainbows to remorse. In 2023, it unveiled a Pride collection that featured 'tuck friendly' female swimsuits with 'extra crotch coverage'. Alongside the girls' swimwear for male bodyparts, Target sold kids' t-shirts with phrases like 'Just Be You And Feel The Love', as well as rainbow onesies, leggings and tutu skirts. The Target website even carried products from a self-described

British transgender Satanist with slogans including 'too queer for here'. It would be difficult to script a crusade more likely to infuriate at least half of America.

Target took the products off display in response to a massive boycott that saw its stock plunge by $14 billion. A year later it had minimalist LGBT merch in selected stores only. So much for pride! Gay rights activists lambasted the volte-face. Hysterical California Governor Gavin Newsom called it a 'systematic attack on the gay community' and 'selling out to extremists'. He tweeted: 'Wake up America. This doesn't stop here. You're black? You're Asian? You're Jewish? You're a woman? You're next.' Really, Gavin? So axing satanic crotch bikinis is a harbinger for the total collapse of all civil rights? Target pleased nobody and upset everybody. It should never have got involved in the first place.

Unfortunately the impulse for brash corporate activism became uncontrollable during the peak years of woke. The tipping point was George Floyd's shocking murder by police officer Derek Chauvin. It was a senseless killing that forced an important reckoning on racism but unfortunately it got completely out of hand. *Everyone* had to say something. Well-meaning demonstrations mutated into violent BLM riots, critical race theory in schools and demands to de-fund the police. Companies found themselves hitched to a wagon that rolled off down a steep slope and sped off the edge of a cliff.

Citigroup's CFO wrote a statement with the words 'I can't breathe' repeated ten times at the top. The boss of Target, who is a middle-aged white man, said the killing had 'unleashed years of pent-up pain'. McDonald's had 'Black Lives Matter' emblazoned beneath the golden arches. Nike went all-out with a huge 'Don't Do It' campaign. Ben & Jerry's said it would settle for nothing less than the 'dismantling of white supremacy'.

Tens of millions poured out of corporate coffers and into BLM. Mark Zuckerberg pledged $10 million to bankroll groups fighting for racial justice but was slammed all over the press by the activists.

Brands coughed up millions but were routinely condemned for lip service. That led to a crazed competition for the grandest gestures, with supermarket aisles reserved for black-owned brands, millions pledged to black-owned businesses and a DEI bonanza. Three-quarters of the top 500 companies on the stock exchange had a Chief Diversity Officer by 2022, compared to less than half a few years earlier. The *New York Post* reported that Coca-Cola put its workers on a course about 'being less white'.

All the while, most ordinary people – neither racist nor activist – carried on living their lives. And then, like a puff of smoke, it was all gone. Companies figured out that most customers would rather not de-fund the police and that the activists will always hate them anyway.

Boobs, bikinis and burgers were back at the Super Bowl because most of the viewers enjoy all of those things. Jaguar's recent outlandish rebrand – fronted by Eurovision-style androgynous weirdos in lurid colours – was met mostly with ridicule or apathy. People voted with their wallets on being browbeaten for bigotry by the guys who sell them clothes or mouthwash – and money is really all any of this has ever been about.

In 2024, before the US election, a whole armada of big firms including Boeing, Walmart, Coors, John Deere, Costco, Ford, Toyota, Harley Davidson and Jack Daniel's all announced plans to scale back DEI programmes or stop funding LGBTQ campaigns. You might wonder why Harley Davidson ever felt it needed a public diversity mission. Now the craze is over, so do they. The trickle became an avalanche after President Trump banned DEI by executive order – pledging a 'merit-based and colour-blind' society. We should all want that, and there are many ugly reasons why we may never get it. But surely we can all agree that it's got nothing to do with McDonald's and Bud Light?

Nothing better illustrates the great renormalisation than the recent saga of a very high-profile advertisement for jeans. Clothing retailer American Eagle has dabbled in all manner of all-inclusive ads for its denims; featuring various plus-sized models of colour and an ensemble of slobs to celebrate 'male body diversity'. But in the summer of 2025 they decided to go decidedly route one again; sparking an almighty furore and the hilarious last desperate gasps of the woke outrage machine.

Superstar actress Sydney Sweeney featured in a flirtatious campaign using the play on words: 'Sydney Sweeney has great jeans.' Most people immediately understood this to be an obvious cheeky reference to Sweeney's genetic blessings and her famous willingness to exhibit them. A rowdy cabal of maniacs on social media, however, began accusing American Eagle of overt racism – and worse.

ABC News interviewed a professor who thundered that Sweeney's ad had 'activated troubling historical associations … specifically, the eugenics movement, which … weaponised the idea of "good genes" to justify white supremacism'. Thousands of livid TikTok users, most of whom clearly had more affinity with the earlier 'body diversity' campaigns, accused the company of 'Nazi propaganda' on the basis that Sweeney is blonde with blue eyes.

It was self-evidently preposterous – and this time everybody knew it. Less than a year earlier Beyoncé had posed in a series of raunchy snaps for Levi's jeans in a marketing blitz that was so successful it raked in $5 million in free media exposure within 48 hours. Millions of people liked it and shared it because she looked great, and it harked back to a time when ads were aspirational. They sold an ideal – something to strive for – instead of a celebration of mediocrity.

In a resounding sign of the rapidly changing times, American Eagle's response to the outcry was to do absolutely nothing. There was no cowering apology, no period of introspection for 'learning and listening', no hasty edits. The deranged lunatics fulminating in Hitlerian hysteria were mercilessly mocked and pilloried. The *Washington Post* published an analysis headlined: 'How American Eagle's Sydney Sweeney ad went wrong'. But it didn't! The company's stock soared by 18 per cent, adding hundreds of millions of dollars to its value.

Popular commentator Kaizen Asiedu, who abandoned the Democrats over their obsession with identity politics and also happens to be black, wrote: 'The Sydney Sweeney ads aren't about white supremacy. There is no "racist undertone", unless you choose to put it there. They're about the end of cancel culture, which demonizes beauty, excellence, and virtue itself. Woke is dead, and beauty is back.' I couldn't have said it better myself!

Chapter 10

WORD POLICE

My preferred pronouns are Hot/Hotter/Hottest. You might not like it or understand it, but it is my truth.

Wokies don't just want to cancel people. They also want to cancel words. 'It's a beautiful thing, the destruction of words,' says the character of Syme in Orwell's dystopian novel *Nineteen Eighty-Four*. Syme's job at the history-re-writing, propaganda-peddling Ministry of Truth is to replace the whole language with a new one called Newspeak. 'Don't you see that the whole aim of Newspeak is to narrow the range of thought?' he asks. 'In the end we shall make thoughtcrime literally impossible, because there will be no words in which to express it.'

Orwell's classic is a seminal warning about tyrannical control of facts and ideas by totalitarian overlords. It has been used to the point of cliché to sound alarm on everything from CCTV cameras to omniscient smart TVs. But not enough attention has been paid to the Ministry of Woke and its rapacious mission of eliminating and redefining words and phrases to make thought criminals of us all.

Up until about five years ago, there was no such thing as your truth or my truth, only THE truth. The whole concept of 'My Truth' is a real-world Orwellian redrafting of history before our eyes. MyTruthers believe what actually happened is irrelevant as long as they felt like it did in their 'lived experience'. To this day Meghan Markle has failed to produce a scrap of evidence for her racism smear on the royal family, but it doesn't matter. Her feelings don't care about your facts.

Oprah Winfrey, who gawped unflinchingly through *that* Meghan interview, is the My Truth pioneer. As the global face of WeightWatchers she often lectured millions of fans on the importance of willpower for shedding pounds – branding weight-loss drugs as the 'easy way out'. She then gave a confessional interview revealing she had in fact taken them herself and was now 'done with the shaming'. So, it was our fault she lied. And that is her truth.

It doesn't stop there. Well-known phrases are now under attack. The term 'black sheep' has been used for centuries to describe a member of a group who doesn't quite fit in or is otherwise scapegoated. Meghan's stress ball Prince Harry is the black sheep of the royal family because he is a selfish twerp. Cristiano Ronaldo said in his explosive interview with me that Manchester United had made him a black sheep by blaming him for all their failures. But according to the woke dictionary, black sheep is now a racial slur.

Joseph Smith, an 'anti-racism trainer', told Canada's national broadcaster CBC: '[It] connotes evil, distrust, lack of intelligence, ignorance, a lack of beauty – the absence of white.' That would be awful – but it doesn't. It comes from shepherds complaining about having literal black sheep in their flocks because the dark wool couldn't be dyed and the animal was worth less money. Several British police forces nonetheless added it to a diversity rulebook which blacklisted the phrase alongside several others – including, unbelievably, 'blacklist'.

Fields are problematic now too. That's right – fields. Reporters on assignment are described as working in the field. Scientists, students and researchers have a field of study. They conduct fieldwork when they interview people or study biology in the wild.

The University of Southern California banned the word as 'anti-Black' on the basis that slaves and migrants also worked in fields. Its Field Department was rebranded as the Practicum Education Department and students were told: 'Our goal is not just to change language but to honour and acknowledge inclusion and reject white supremacy, anti-immigrant and anti-blackness ideologies.' No sane individual in human history has ever associated the word 'field' with white supremacy. And Orwell's fabled tyrants never got close to anything so grotesquely ridiculous.

Diversity trainers might accuse me of having a blind spot when it comes to this imaginary oppression. But that would be offensive too. Disability rights activist Julie Cashman told CBC: 'I can see that being offensive to people who can't see.' On that basis I think Cashman boasting about her ability to see is a bit tone deaf. And that will cost me another coin in the swear jar because Cashman thinks 'tone deaf' alienates deaf people and should instead be replaced by 'musically disinclined'.

An essay in *Harvard Business Review* adds 'stupid', 'insane', 'crazy', 'lame' and 'dumb' to this disability-smearing hitlist, explaining: 'You have (unknowingly or not) participated in spreading ableist language.' Lydia X. Z. Brown, a 'disability justice advocate', concluded: 'When someone tells you that something is disrespectful, you don't have to understand why they are hurt. Just that they are.' My truth again. Suffice it to say I think this is stupid, insane, crazy, lame and dumb.

As always, men have been misidentified as a major problem. The European Union took umbrage with the phrases tradesman, manpower, and man on the street. Politico banned manhunt. California's Berkeley City Council ditched man hours and manholes – because sisters can plunge into sewers, too.

The founding father (or non-birthing parent) of this movement was obviously Justin Trudeau, who rudely interrupted a young woman's question about the future of mankind – because 'we like to say peoplekind'.

It can all get out of hand very quickly, not least because the word 'woman' contains the word 'man'. Democratic Congresswoman Jan Schakowsky told a committee hearing in February that fewer women are taking manufacturing jobs because the word 'sounds like a guy'. She did not explain why so many manicurists are women. And I highly recommend she runs for re-election on changing it to 'personfacturing' so we never have to hear from her again.

In October 2022, an opening monologue for my show began like this: *'Ladies and gentlemen, these are difficult times for Britain. Our neediest people are struggling to keep up with brutal rises in energy bills. Rocketing rents could leave some people homeless. Now mortgage rates are exploding too. Millions of young people have no hope of ever owning their own homes without the bank of mom and dad.*

'Caucasian boys, many of them raised in our most deprived neighbourhoods, are now the worst-performing demographic for getting university places. And today, charities are warning the disabled and handicapped will be the worst-hit by the government's benefit cuts, fuelling yet another split in [Prime Minister] Liz Truss's cabinet. Meanwhile, refugees and economic migrants continue to cross the channel in small boats – a crisis the Home Secretary admits is out of control.'

All of that was true. But my main point was to highlight an 18-page 'Inclusive Language Guide' sent to regional councils that outlawed almost every noun I used. Authorities were warned to stop using ladies and gentlemen, neediest, deprived, disabled and handicapped, economic migrants and homeless. All of them were deemed offensive.

Is it any wonder they are doing such a dismal job of solving people's real-world problems when they are so preoccupied with fighting over what to call the people?

'Ladies and gentlemen' was replaced in the guide by 'welcome, everyone' to avoid upsetting anybody who's in between.

Depressingly this policy has also now been adopted by British Airways, whose pilots now welcome me aboard with the bleak term 'passengers'. Again this is to protect the rights of people who are neither ladies nor gentlemen. But what about my right, as a gentleman, to feel good about myself? A gentleman cruises the rarefied air en route to exotic climes or power meetings. A passenger is a burdensome lump.

I often fly British Airways to California, where I own a home and live for part of the year. The ultra-woke governor Gavin Newsom has taken extreme positions on everything from race quotas to puberty blockers in schools, which is a whole other story. California has a visibly devastating homelessness problem, which has got exponentially worse despite Newsom spending a mind-blowing $24 billion on trying to end it.

Instead it has simply ended referring to homeless people as homeless. Preferred terms are 'unhoused' – tents can be homes, technically – and 'individuals experiencing homelessness'. The *Associated Press Stylebook* also now favours 'people without housing' as this is 'person-first language' that avoids focusing on only one aspect of their identity. The problem is that homeless people are pretty damn focused on one aspect of their identity – being homeless. They would rather we identify a home for them.

Identity obsession is at the heart of most of this language-mangling. Everything is about the all-important 'me' and how *my* personal choices are impacted by everybody else. How *my* truth is most important. The corruption of language provides endless new opportunities to indulge in the favourite woke pastime – being offended. And at the same time it insidiously imposes a very specific worldview on a whole load of people who might have a different one altogether. That is why it is worth resisting – no matter how trivial it appears on the surface.

Pronouns briefly took over the world. It became impossible to read an email, glance at a name badge or look at a social media bio without seeing 'he/him', 'she/her' or 'they/them'. At first it was a voluntary act of politeness, made contagious by the desire to showcase moral superiority.

Then came mandates. Civil servants were urged to add pronouns to official emails and big employers like the BBC told workers it was a 'small, proactive step that we can all take to help create a more inclusive workplace'. Halifax Bank doled out 'inclusive' pronoun name badges to staff in their branches and told anyone who didn't like it to close their account. Inclusive – but only if you want to play the pronoun game.

Then-Vice President Kamala Harris infamously began a roundtable meeting with disability activists by announcing: 'I am Kamala Harris. My pronouns are she and her. I am a woman sitting at the table wearing a blue suit.'

The last part was for the benefit of blind guests, who clearly do need help establishing their surroundings. But everyone on earth knows that she is a woman and that women are referred to as 'she' and 'her'. The clip resurfaced and was shared millions of times in the election campaign because it shows the surreal absurdity of the whole idea and how readily and gleefully she went along with it.

If you ask someone for their pronouns, you can only be doing one of two things. Either you are saying that you can't work out what their sex is, which most people would find quite rude. Or you are deliberately declaring that you believe in gender identity politics and expect everyone else to do the same.

Announcing your own pronouns has no practical purpose whatsoever because we only use them to talk *about* other people – not to them. It's nothing more than a declaration of your virtue and a test of theirs. That is why my preferred pronouns are Hot/Hotter/Hottest. You might not like it or understand it, but it is my truth.

The onslaught of gender-neutral phrases is essential to the woke ideology, which needs to overturn centuries of innate wisdom to convince the human race that biology and identity are equal. Universities have taken up this challenge with vim.

The University of Greenwich suggested boyfriend or girlfriend become 'partner', Manchester University's language guide replaced mother or father with 'guardian' and Leeds University went with the dismal 'carer'. The British NHS has faced endless negative headlines about ludicrous directives to replace words like breastfeeding and mother with 'chestfeeding' and 'birthing parent'. At one point it reportedly warned staff that using the wrong gendered language is a 'microaggression', which can lead to post-traumatic stress disorder.

Just as nobody has ever been traumatised by a pronoun, no student has yet been thrown out of class for saying 'mother'. No doctors have been struck off for using the wrong pronouns, as far as I'm aware. But that's not really the point. It's about a whole movement of activists and bureaucrats trying to normalise the fundamentally abnormal by stealth.

If you have to hesitate before using perfectly ordinary words then somebody else's niche worldview has already been stamped on your brain. Liberals downplay it, of course. They say it's no big deal, just a load of wonks doing silly academic stuff. To which I say, OK, fine – why waste public money on indulging it?

Forget the gender madness, the whole thing is just so bleakly joyless. Mother, father, sister, brother, boyfriend, girlfriend – all of these words evoke love and warmth. Who the hell wants to be a caregiving spouse?

This corruption of language has even seeped into our classic literature. Roald Dahl's joyful books have delighted children around the world for generations. Many have become smash hit movies. His stories and characters are gloriously grisly, mischievous and surprising – all jam-packed with deliciously wicked wit. Puffin, the late author's publisher, decided they were also dangerously offensive. Dystopian sounding 'sensitivity readers' were hired to ransack Dahl's works to ensure the books 'can continue to be enjoyed by all today'. Hundreds of changes were made and whole passages never written by Dahl were added in their place. It is wanton cultural vandalism.

The cloud men in *James and the Giant Peach* became 'cloud people' – perhaps to protect the non-binary clouds. Oompa Loompas in *Charlie and the Chocolate Factory* were described by Dahl as 'small men' but rewritten as 'small people' – because small men can identify as small women. The black tractors in *Fantastic Mr Fox* had their colour removed, as if simply mentioning the colour of an inanimate object is now racist.

Augustus Gloop, Wonka's fabled glutton, was no longer described as 'fat'. Miss Trunchbull, Fat Aunt Sponge and Mrs Twit were also relieved of various body-shaming remarks on their appearance. In a passage explaining how The Witches are bald beneath their wigs, a disclaimer was added to explain: 'There are plenty of other reasons why women might wear wigs and there is certainly nothing wrong with that.'

The sensitivity readers even erased 'double chin' from a passage in *The Twits* which originally said: 'You can have a wonky nose and a crooked mouth and a double chin and stick-out teeth.' That edit was probably about fat-shaming. But what about shaming people for wonky noses, crooked mouths and stick-out teeth? That's all fine?

At some point the wonky-nosed community might demand protections. Stephen Fry, Owen Wilson and Sylvester Stallone could start a wonky nose positivity movement and decry the wonky nose shaming in our culture. Once you head off down this slippery slope there is really no turning back.

The logical endpoint is a lot of empty pages or a very boring world. Author Salman Rushdie called it 'absurd censorship'. He survived a multi-decade Fatwa and a stabbing attack over his novel *The Satanic Verses* but never gave up writing and speaking his mind. How outrageously insulting that the industry and art form he sacrificed everything for has succumbed to censorship over the gender of little orange chocolatiers.

'Shaming' is a prime example of the important companion to word cancellation – let's call it *define* intervention. Sometimes words are too useful to be erased. Instead they are reclaimed and personfactured into something bearing no resemblance to the original meaning. This is always to provide new ways of expressing offence.

Anything that counters the 'overweight is great' lie previously sponsored by Lizzo, Adele and Oprah is filed under fat shaming. Body positivity also spawned 'food shaming', which is making someone feel guilty about their meal choice. 'Gift shaming' is moaning about derivative or cheap presents. 'Work shaming' is shunning those colleagues who – five years after the pandemic – remain at home in their underpants. None of this is actual 'shaming'. And it also deflects all blame from the real culprits – people who eat too much, give crap gifts and never go to work.

'Violence' used to mean physical acts of aggression that are intended to hurt someone. Now words are violence, history is violence, ignorance is violence. The UN decided that 'exclusion is violence'. The Anti-Violence Project added that 'Trans Exclusionary Radical Feminism is violence.'

Celebrities including singer Alicia Keys helped to popularise 'silence is violence' during the BLM protests. That one really caught fire because it rhymes. But it's not true. It also helped power the moral panic that led to burger joints and supermarkets backing de-fund the police. Lots of things can be unpleasant and they may even cause violence but, seriously, we learn about the bone-breaking ability of sticks and stones as toddlers. For the record, none of the above causes 'trauma' either. And when it comes to celebrities weighing in on politics, silence is golden.

Thankfully, the end is nigh for the language police. Like most authoritarians through history they overreached and got tangled up in their own traps. There is an incredible viral video of a US socialist convention descending into complete chaos as one language sin leads to another. A delegate interrupts the speaker to say: 'Quick point of personal privilege. Um, guys, first of all, James Jackson, Sacramento, he/him. I just want to say, can we please keep the chatter to the minimum? I'm one of the people who's very, very prone to sensory overload.'

The speaker tries to carry on before another furious delegate interrupts to bellow: 'Do not use gendered language to address everyone!' He was triggered by the use of 'guys', and the sensory overload guy interrupts the ensuing melee to say his anxiety has been triggered by the argument about triggering.

CNN's national correspondent reported on the LGBT blowback to Bud Light's handling of the Dylan Mulvaney fiasco by explaining: 'He, of course, is the transgender person they were going to sponsor ... they didn't like how Bud Light didn't stand by him after all this.' Did you spot the fatal error?

The next day anchor Kate Bolduan, stern-faced as though announcing a national emergency, said: 'Yesterday, in a segment about transgender influencer Dylan Mulvaney, who was featured in Bud Light's recent campaign, she was mistakenly referred to by the wrong pronouns ... we apologise for that error.' The problem with setting impossible standards for other people is that they are impossible for you, too.

For decades British people were encouraged to use the acronym BAME to refer to black, asian and minority ethnic people. Its harmless roots were the 1970s anti-racism movement, in which many different non-white groups united to protest very genuine racism problems. As TV presenters and writers we were told to use it. But in the slipstream of the post-2020 race frenzy, it was cancelled. All the major broadcasters announced as one that BAME was banished because it failed to recognise individual identities and it was offensive to lump all ethnic minorities together.

Suddenly a load of charities with BAME in their names were on the naughty step, despite being created by BAME people to help BAME people. And when it comes to bundling groups together to make a political point, nobody does it better than the moral crusaders themselves.

Take the word 'Latinx'; another Newspeak atrocity that is now being abolished. It was amplified by the likes of Alexandria Ocasio-Cortez and Kamala Harris as a gender-neutral form of Latino. Half of all Democrats in the last Congress used it on social media – compared to zero Republicans.

The campaign failed, as they did. A series of polls found that a thumping majority of actual Hispanics either despise the term or have no idea what it means. Latinos flocked to Trump in the presidential election, even as he railed against illegal immigration and threatened mass deportations to Latin American countries. Maybe throwing socially conservative, family-first Catholics into the oppressed minority bucket alongside trans activists was always as dumb as it sounds.

Governor Newsom's hilarious recent attempts to prove he was actually never woke at all included the brazen claim that he'd never used the word Latinx. 'By the way, not one person ever in my office has ever used the word Latinx,' he said. 'I just didn't even know where it came from. What are people talking about?' They are talking about you, Gavin! A whole slew of clips and tweets emerged very quickly showing the ghastly governor used the term Latinx incessantly, including a lament of how '#COVID19 disproportionately impacts the Latinx community'.

Trump's own language has become a marker for the gradual recovery of normal words. A politician caught swearing on a hot mic used to be a media scandal. When Joe Biden, then vice-president, told Obama 'this is a big fucking deal' it made global headlines for days. Trump, on the other hand, drops f-bombs more often than he does the exploding military kind – and sometimes at the same time. Shortly after sanctioning the US attack on Iran's nuclear facilities and announcing Israel and Iran had agreed a ceasefire in their short war, Trump angrily denounced news of fresh bombing by telling reporters: 'They don't know what the fuck they are doing.'

Whether a US president should curse in public is a debatable matter of taste. But there is no doubt his whole speaking style – blunt, punchy, coarse and simple – comes off as much more authentic than the pronoun-wielding Latinx peddlers. It's one of the main ways in which he's always been able to appeal to blue-collar workers.

Roald Dahl's original words, in all their double-chinned glory, are now back on sale. Copies of the sinful texts started popping up on eBay at exorbitant prices and even liberal darlings like Emma Thompson, who starred in the big screen version of *Matilda*, joined the censorship criticism. Puffin caved and released the unedited books as a 'Classic Collection'.

The UK government got fed up with headlines about 'chestfeeders' and instructed the NHS to go back to using plain English. Cate Blanchett, an avowed feminist who has bemoaned her 'white privilege', disavowed the MyTruthers by saying: 'I mean, the truth is the truth, isn't it?' And Oscar-winning actor Sean Penn got to the nub of the matter when he told the Oxford Union: 'I don't know how you talk about pronouns when babies are getting fucking vaporised on the front line in Ukraine.' Exactly.

If you have looked at social media at all in the last couple of years, you will know the extent to which the language-mangling era is over. Elon Musk's transformation of Twitter into X has triggered an explosion of free speech fundamentalism and the other platforms have followed his lead. Not all of it is great for the standard of public discourse. A university study found that use of the word 'retard' has suddenly tripled on X, for example. But with every reaction, there is an overreaction. There are actual laws to safeguard against genuine harassment and abuse without needing to make thought crimes out of fields.

Chapter 11

ENVIRO-MENTALISTS

*If I was the public face of a puritanical protest
movement, on the eve of planned civil unrest, I'd
probably lay off the Chilean grapes and take a bus.*

'The World Transformed' is a conference for Britain's
radical left. Fleabitten communists, hangry vegans and
sandal-wearing students gather beneath vivid Soviet-style
banners to rally for – in their words – a 'socialist utopia'.
The whole thing looks like a battle re-enactment, and the
sort of place where people lose friends – or teeth – over
whether they're for Marx or Mao. In 2023, the delegates
wanted to know why, all around the world, the far left
keeps losing. Britain's most notorious climate activist
Roger Hallam stepped up with an answer: 'The problem,'
he said, 'is that you're all fucking cunts.'

Hallam is a weathered, beardy old Marxist who used to
be an organic farmer and still looks like one. The great
irony of his incisive diagnosis is that he might well be
Britain's biggest ... cretin. Hallam is a professional

protester who spawned not only Extinction Rebellion but its ugly sisters Just Stop Oil and Insulate Britain.

For several years they waged a performative guerrilla war across the UK that spread to the US, Australia and beyond. They blocked roads, forced airports to cancel flights, camped out for days in public squares. Anything to irritate as many people as possible, all at once.

For some reason this did not save the planet and Hallam's army of crusty munchkins moved on to wrecking sports events and throwing paint around. Barely a week passed without an increasingly outrageous stunt. At one point, London's Met Police was spending more than £37 million a year on Extinction Rebellion protests, even as the public howled about their soft touch strategy in failing to deal with them.

They have suddenly all gone very quiet. Extinction Rebellion says it is scaling back mass public disruption to be more 'inclusive'. Many smaller copycat groups have followed them into retreat. Media coverage of nose-ringed vagrants glueing themselves to fences has dropped off a cliff. And Roger Hallam is now in jail.

He was walloped with a five-year sentence for masterminding the shutdown of London's biggest motorway in what he hoped would be the worst disruption in 'modern history'. In England, laws have now been toughened up so that police can intervene before the chaos instead of five days later. But the real reason for the inglorious unravelling of these hypocritical dingbats is actually quite simple. Roger Hallam knew it all along. Absolutely everybody hates them.

Amanda Bishop is not a typical *Uncensored* guest. She's a gardener and mother of three from a quiet suburb. But on the day she came to my studio she had an extraordinary story to tell. She had missed her mother's funeral that morning because climate protesters had blocked the roads, which at one point they were doing in cities around the world on a monthly basis.

The family eventually had to make do with a rushed 10-minute service and her mother's best friend missed it altogether. On the opposite side of my desk were two Just Stop Oil supporters – Hannah Hunt and Eden Lazarus – who banged on about the government being the real criminals. Amanda stared them down and hit the nail on the head: 'You are not winning hearts and minds. All you are doing is antagonising, annoying and breaking the law.' For every act of road-blocking petulance there were hundreds of Amanda Bishops. And thousands of ordinary people just trying to get to work, drop their children at school or make it to their medical appointments.

Five months later, Hannah and Eden turned up in the news again as they were forced by a court to pay £1,000 to the National Gallery for glueing themselves to *The Hay Wain*, one of the UK's most famous paintings. Not only was this spectacularly stupid, it was also painfully unoriginal.

Hundreds have glued their hands to roads. A former Paralympian glued himself to the roof of an aeroplane. Three protesters were convicted for glueing themselves to a climate-friendly electric commuter train in London. And everybody in the world must have seen at least one photograph of a sulking pink-haired pest affixed to a masterpiece.

In a few frenzied months in 2022, brattish vandals bonded themselves to a Picasso in Australia, a Botticelli in Italy and a Raphael in Germany. Glue-natics later threw soup at Van Gogh's *Sunflowers* in London before sticking themselves to the wall. Superglue may have been the weapon of choice for Just Stop Oil in the war against its own popularity but it is, regrettably, made from synthetic chemicals derived from oil.

Protest groups are supposed to rally popular support in order to pressure governments into acting on their concerns. That's how the whole thing works. No strategy has been more self-destructive and moronic than wrecking sporting events, where thousands of people gather to enjoy themselves and forget about everything else. And no sport has been left unsullied by the orange-shirted menaces.

In 2022, a greasy looking Just Stop Oil protester jumped onto the pitch and bound himself to the goalpost at an Everton Premier League match. He had already spent time in jail for glueing himself to the M25 motorway, causing hours of delays for thousands of people. His message proved so popular with the crowd that another fan ran onto the pitch and punched him in the stomach as he was eventually carried away. Sadly, it was only the beginning.

Six tangerine tyrants ran onto the racetrack at the British Grand Prix in 2023, where Formula 1 cars belt along at 200 mph. Any driver swerving to miss them could have died in a fireball, not to mention the safety stewards who dashed in to prevent the activists being mowed down by a speeding 2,000 lb box of gasoline.

British racing legend Sir Lewis Hamilton irresponsibly defended Just Stop Oil before later clarifying that they should protest away from the track. In other words, they are welcome to block you from getting to work in the morning just as long as they don't bother Formula 1, a globe-traversing festival of machinery that is probably the world's biggest advertisement for oil.

Protesters later raided a PGA golf championship in Connecticut, the storied Wimbledon tennis championship, the US Open in New York and an NBA game in Minnesota. British police made a whopping 118 arrests when a whole swarm of enviro-gnats descended on the world-famous Grand National horse race.

The woeful self-sabotaging lunacy of the whole campaign was encapsulated by one moronic student's invasion of the World Snooker Championship. Edred Whittingham (why do they always sound like stilted aristocrats from a Jane Austen novel?) mounted the table, tossed orange powder everywhere and started shrieking dementedly.

Snooker audiences tend to be well-behaved working-class people in their prime years. Sometimes they nap. But this crowd began baying like a raging mob, shouting 'get him off' while the TV commentator lamented the 'terrible, terrible scenes'. I would bet every cent in Elon Musk's bank account that precisely none of them – nor any of the millions who saw it on TV – watched this performance and decided to start cutting their carbon emissions as a result.

Mr Whittingham later set off an orange powder-loaded fire extinguisher at his own graduation ceremony before being dragged off, smirking, by police. He said in a statement: 'What use is an education if society is collapsing around you?' I'd agree that his education was a terrible waste of his parents' money – just not for the reason he thinks.

In June 2023, I was at Lord's Cricket Ground to witness a masterclass. England's Jonny Bairstow displayed his poise, strength, discipline and dexterity in a world-class performance that delighted supporters from both sides and won plaudits across the globe. Readers in the US will be relieved to discover it had absolutely nothing to do with cricket.

Two powder-throwing protesters (a third had been stopped by security) rushed the pitch, hell-bent on ruining the Test match as they'd ruined so many other national events. Bairstow calmly lifted up the chief irritant and carried him – horizontal and helpless – all the way off the pitch. He made it look as effortless and tedious as putting away the ironing board. Play resumed after about 20 minutes.

Anybody who knows anything about cricket will attest that a spot of light drizzle in a neighbouring village can suspend a match for longer than that – so the joke really was on them. And the crowd loved it because Bairstow did what hundreds of police officers in thousands of viral clips had bafflingly failed to do.

Simmering frustration with this endless cycle of disruption and indulgence inevitably boiled over into a very literal backlash. Police have to follow all sorts of rules: some of them are very justified rules about the democratic right to protest. But mostly they have to send enough officers to manage a giant traffic jam and arrest protesters without injuring them or being injured themselves.

Irate commuters eventually decided they simply did not have time to wait for Lady Justice. Protesters found themselves dragged off roads, yanked from the tops of trains and denuded of their banners by furious members of the public who just wanted to get to work. A man in London charged through a traffic-stopping march like a raging bull; a woman in Germany hauled activists off the road by their hair; truckers near Brisbane Airport lugged them aside by the actual scruffs of their necks. All were cheered on by millions as the videos went viral. The vandals had been cosplaying as revolutionaries but found themselves on the receiving end of a genuine global uprising – against them!

You may have noticed that I have not once mentioned climate science in this chronicle of derangement. Neither did most of the many thousands of news reports about the commotion. Protesters bleated about 'raising awareness' and 'starting a conversation' but in reality they only raised awareness of their own imbecility and started conversations about how selfish they are.

At the peak of the frenzy a colossal 74 per cent of British adults said they were *already* worried about climate change. Every major political party agreed and had varying plans to spend billions on fixing it. More than 97 per cent of publishing scientists agree that humans are warming up the planet with serious consequences that need attention. These are numbers that would make Kim Jong-un blush. So what exactly was the point?

Protest against governments for not doing enough, if you like. Protest against big companies for cutting costs with cheap plastic that festers in landfills for 500 years. Protest against the oil companies who gaslight motorists about their great love of solar panels. At least all of that makes sense. But breaking the law to harm ordinary working people who have absolutely no choice but to drive to work? That's just idiocy. It has alienated many more people than it has persuaded. The disruptors are really just privileged birdbrains searching for an identity-defining purpose and then deciding that their purpose is more important than everybody else's right to live their lives.

The whole movement sits somewhere between religious fundamentalism and mental illness. It takes a genuine disorder, even if it's plain old narcissism, to believe life on earth faces imminent extinction by incineration and that you alone can save it by stapling your face to a bus. The religious bent comes from the all-out moral despotism. We, the enlightened few, have the final answer and compromise is intolerable.

The reality is that even climate change experts are engaged in vigorous debates about the speed and scope of solutions for man-made global warming. I'm not a science-denier. I believe it's a fundamental right and a necessity for future generations to be raised in a world with breathable air, lustrous forests and abundant clean water.

I just don't think it's remotely feasible for every fossil fuel to be instantly banned without collapsing the economy and civilisation as we know it. Plenty of better-informed people agree. And there's a key difference between the attention-seekers and real-life fundamentalists. Those in the latter camp may be bonkers, but they do tend to practise what they preach.

The Extinction Rebellion co-founder Gail Bradbrook was photographed at a swanky supermarket on the eve of a massive four-day protest to demand an immediate 'end to the fossil fuel era' (plus 'reparations' for climate damage, of course). Her shopping basket was laden with plastic-wrapped produce that had flown a total of 17,000 miles to reach her local convenience store and she duly loaded it all into her fume-blasting diesel car for the short ride home. All very normal behaviour. But if I was the public face of a puritanical protest movement, on the eve of planned civil unrest, I'd probably lay off the Chilean grapes and take a bus.

Vegan *Guardian* bore George Monbiot slammed me online for highlighting London's air pollution problem, which makes me ill and sluggish at various times every year, on the basis that I have 'spent years attacking and insulting people who have tried to address the causes of air pollution'. But I haven't. I've spent years insulting vandals who target regular working people and vegan hypocrites who show up to my live TV interviews wearing shoes made from murdered cows. Sound familiar, George?

The worst offenders, though, are much higher in the celebrity food chain – usually about 35,000 ft higher. They include my old pals Harry and Meghan, who have made incessant environmental lecturing a core strategy in their waning quest for relevance. 'There is a ticking clock on our planet,' they said in a rousing joint statement, adding: 'Let's save it. Let's do our part.'

Harry and Meghan use private jets as often as I use black cabs. Years of rampant five-star globetrotting include privately jetting for holidays at Elton John's French palace and on a remote Caribbean island, as well as to a Katy Perry concert in Las Vegas. Flying in a private jet for a single hour releases more carbon dioxide than an average person does in an entire year, according to experts at a Swedish university. What Harry and Meghan meant to say was: 'You save it. You do your part. We'll send you a postcard.'

Oscar-winning heart-throb Leonardo DiCaprio is a first-class actor and an A-List Hollywood hypocrite. In the summer of 2023, he was snapped soaking up the sun on four different superyachts. Besides being a splendid way to tan, superyachts spew sewage into the sea and pump out copious amounts of carbon with engines and air conditioning throbbing 24/7.

DiCaprio, a UN climate change ambassador, once flew 4,000 miles from Cannes to New York on a private jet – to receive an award for his environmental activism. After collecting his gong he promptly reboarded the jet and flew straight back to France. And as wildfires raged across Los Angeles in January this year, a tragedy that activists say was exacerbated by global warming, DiCaprio quickly fled Hollywood. No 'green awards' for guessing the mode of transport.

It's an inconvenient truth that Al Gore has probably clocked up more air miles than George Clooney in *Up in the Air*, and that I suspect climate envoy John Kerry has spent as much time on Mars as he has inside a commercial economy cabin. All of these high-profile hypocrites claim their travel is 'carbon neutral' because they buy 'carbon offsets'.

Elton John said he personally paid to 'offset' Harry and Meghan's trip to his chateau; one of four private flights they had taken in 11 days. But carbon offsets are the very definition of what President Trump calls a 'green new scam'. Companies draw a line around a forest on a map, claim they're now protecting it and then sell off portions of the carbon sucked in by the trees to guilty travellers.

This is often understood to be planting trees but they're not even doing that. In most cases the trees were there already and the seller is literally just speculating on how bad it would be if they were cut down. It's exactly like a mob boss charging you for security outside your family business after menacing that it would be terrible if something should happen to it.

Clearly, the lesson is that there are no quick fixes and that endlessly berating people as environmental sinners is a zero-sum game. Greta 'you have stolen my dreams' Thunberg has promoted the myth that selfish boomers are torching the planet while saintly young victims are melting in their selfishness-fuelled furnace. But that's wrong, too.

Gen Z worships people like the Kardashians and Kylie Jenner, whose social media is flooded with photos of their lavish private jet use. This demographic are also obsessed with Bitcoin; the digital cryptocurrency whose creation takes so much computer power and electricity that its emissions are bigger than the entire nation of New Zealand. And presumably they are interested in Bitcoin because they want to get rich quickly, which will allow them to emulate the Kardashians and fly in a private jet.

This green scare is coming to an abrupt end now. One of the big stories of the US election was the drift of young voters to Donald Trump, who yanked the US out of the Paris Climate Agreement and summarised his climate change policy as 'Drill, baby, drill'. Politicians now rarely grandstand about it at all.

Greta's own personal downfall has mirrored its disappearance. In 2019, she was named *Time Magazine's* youngest ever Person of the Year. Adulating media spoke of the 'Greta Effect' in recruiting a mass movement of young eco warriors. She was universally acclaimed by powerful figures including no less than Barack Obama and Pope Francis. But if you ever see Greta on social media now, it's either shrieking at an anti-Israel protest or as the butt of a joke. The US President mocks her 'anger management problem'.

And what became of Greta's global army of climate-conscious school strikers? You can find them on TikTok, showing off the entire wardrobe of brand-new single-use clothes they ship from China on a monthly basis. Or buying disposable crap that arrives within 24 hours in a Russian doll of plastic-loaded cardboard boxes, absolutely all of which is destined to end up inside a landfill or a whale.

I've waged a private war on loudmouth vegans for several years now. I don't really care what people eat or choose not to eat, but I do object to other people telling me to eat what they eat or go to hell. You can identify a vegan easily based on their ghostly skin and languid demeanour. But generally they'll have announced it within moments of meeting you anyway, like an environmental pronoun.

Outshone by their carbon-crazed cousins, militant vegans began raiding supermarkets to pour all of the milk on the floor at the peak of the cost-of-living crisis. A week of coordinated mass tantrums saw them blockade dairy facilities and spray white paint all over the historic walls beside Big Ben.

I found all of this to be outrageously insulting and decided to outrageously insult the Animal Rebellion spokeswoman by eating a Big Mac in front of her, live on air. Ofcom received 100 formal complaints. The various videos on YouTube received many millions of views with resoundingly supportive feedback – for me.

Hectoring and hypocrisy are again the main issues I have. The vegan millennial meal of choice is avocado toast with an almond milk latte. But large-scale production of both avocados and almonds is disastrous for the environment. They don't like to talk about that, so I will.

First, it decimates bees, without which there would be no flowers or crops. Billions of bees are trucked across the US to pollinate harvests in places where they would really rather not be hanging out. They sadly show their disapproval by dying very shortly afterwards. Secondly, both almond and avocado trees gulp preposterous quantities of water from already-parched lands. It takes four litres of water to grow one single almond and 150 almonds to make a single carton of almond milk. An avocado tree inhales 320 litres of water to produce just one avocado. Every single order of Instagram's most ubiquitous brunch choice has ingested enough water to hydrate a child for a year. But *I'm* the monster because I like cheese?

Admittedly, it did briefly seem like I was losing the war on veganism, but I have now emerged like Lazarus from my tomb. Sales of 'plant-based' fake meats have recently plunged by 21 per cent, leading to many of them being withdrawn from the shelves. The number of people identifying as vegan has fallen by 28 per cent in Europe and participation in 'Veganuary' – a month-long commitment to gruel at the beginning of the year – is now declining.

Young people are actually eating more meat now because the latest fad is maximum protein and 'caveman' diets that shun the preservatives and chemicals in processed foods. Caveman is a trend I feel entirely comfortable with. And for the record, it is possible to oppose animal cruelty and factory farming – as I do – without being an aggressive vegan. Just as it's clearly possible for aggressive vegans to murder bees and steal all our water.

Nobody should celebrate the destruction of nature. It's both a precious bond to our ancestral roots and the basis of all life itself. We're demonstrably racing through our stocks of clean air, productive soil, wetlands and forests. None of this is a good thing at all. But that's precisely why I do celebrate the gradual reclaiming of this cause from radical self-obsessed zealots with net-zero brain cells.

It was always more about their personal search for meaning than it was about being green. They said they were saving the world, but they were really saving themselves. As the saying goes, you won't find the answers at the bottom of a bottle – of superglue. The magazine that originally reported on Roger Hallam's expletive-laden verdict on his leftist peers included an interview with details of his big new plans to fight this demise – and fight Trump – from behind bars. I sincerely hope he doesn't – for the sake of the planet.

Chapter 12

ROYAL RUCTIONS

The British monarchy ... has survived woke,
and survived the Sussexes, the way it inexorably
survives every crisis.

'I struggle even to imagine Britain without our Queen. But with great sadness, we now have to imagine it, because the moment we've all been dreading has finally come.' Just minutes after Buckingham Palace formally announced the passing of Queen Elizabeth II on 8 September 2022, I opened my show with a three-minute tribute that had been several decades in the making. 'The Greatest of Britons,' I said. 'When Her Majesty the Queen died this afternoon in Balmoral, a little piece of us all died with her.' It was a surreal day, filled with the heaviness and jarring sense of focus that comes with a sudden emergency. We'd all had many years to prepare for it and yet nobody knew quite how to feel.

The late Queen was the ultimate antidote to a world gone nuts. For 70 years she reigned with quiet dignity and wry wisdom. Wars raged, governments imploded, markets crashed; cars replaced horses, phones became computers, the web connected everything before sending everybody insane. And all the while, our ever-present monarch sat atop the frenzy as an enduring symbol of comforting consistency.

Even the royal-bashing posers and redcoat-bashing Americans generally gave the late Queen a pass. Nobody really had a bad word to say about her. More than a quarter of a million people of all ages and races lined up to pay tribute as she lay in state, joining a queue that stretched for 10 miles and peaked at 24 hours' waiting time. Many more were told not to turn up. Tributes poured in for days from every corner of the planet and the world's media was transfixed. Very few people in modern history have commanded attention and affection the way she did. Few will ever do so again.

In what we now know to be her very final days, the Queen dragged herself from her deathbed to formally appoint the new Prime Minister, Liz Truss. The Queen looked frail and delicate in those photographs; one outstretched hand was bruised and the other held a walking stick. But she had the same toothy, beaming smile as always and found the energy to make classically British wisecracks about the torrid late summer weather.

At a time when many healthy young people were openly fuming about returning to the office after Covid, this was quite a riposte. She died just two days later. And that meeting became Liz Truss' only unblemished act in a historically disastrous 49 days as Prime Minister; memorably losing a longevity contest to a fresh lettuce.

Many people fretted about the future of the monarchy without its seemingly eternal figurehead. And there is no doubt the royal family has taken a battering. The royals had to rapidly reboot the dated way they communicate private matters for social media followers who demand constant all-access updates and propel wild theories to fill any voids.

They faced down a five-year onslaught from the Sussex separatists, who attacked the institution as a cruel and racist anachronism, in my view to boost their own brand. But the monarchy is doing what monarchy does – enduring, calmly above the fray. Brand Sussex, meanwhile, is now about as popular as Ebola. The survival of the royals in the face of their barrage is a grand repudiation of the whole cult of frivolous celebrity and the divisive trends of race-baiting and historical apologism. If you come for the king, you'd better not miss.

It's now clear that Harry and Meghan's infamous Oprah whine-a-thon came at the very apex of woke insanity. Everybody was assumed guilty until proven innocent, especially on socially sensitive matters like race or mental health. Self-certifying as a victim meant *your* truth was gospel and facts be damned.

Damaging allegations about the royal family will always make global news, but I don't think the reaction would be anywhere near as unquestioning and sympathetic if the same interview happened today. Riding this wave of self-pitying martyrdom may have been the only smart thing the Sussexes have ever done. But waves have to break in the end – and so does the public's patience with liars.

None of Harry and Meghan's most sensational accusations of royal racism – the charge that unnamed royals were worried about their future son's skin colour, nor Meghan's claim that she was denied help for suicidal thoughts – has ever been supported by a shred of verified independent evidence.

After I was forced to quit *Good Morning Britain* for stating – on the morning after the Oprah interview – that I didn't believe a word Meghan had said, I later discovered she'd demanded my head on a spike in a letter to ITV chiefs, who instructed that I either publicly apologise to Markle or leave my job. Not for a single fleeting moment have I ever regretted defending my right – and everybody else's right – to give an opinion. Nor have I ever thought that she may have been telling the truth. Both *Good Morning Britain* and the Sussexes have watched their ratings tumble ever since.

Six months after my walk of fame, the UK's TV regulator Ofcom ruled that I had every right to disbelieve the Sussexes and to say so. It now seems staggering that it needed an 'investigation' to decide whether journalists have the right to question the veracity of a whining actress, who in my opinion is prone to espousing 'her truth' rather than the actual truth. But that really is how close Britain came to circling the free speech drain in reverence to MyTruth madness.

Still, the main reason for my vindication is nothing to do with any bureaucratic judgement. It's the atrociously treacherous deeds of Harry and Meghan ever since that moment – and the voracious zeal with which the public has come to detest them.

Netflix signed a reported $100 million deal with the renegade royals shortly after Megxit (a phrase which Harry has bizarrely branded 'misogynistic'). Having already given an explosive tell-all interview to Oprah, who as far as we know paid them nothing, the expectation was for massive revelations.

Their self-titled documentary series – two years in the making – was to be spread across six hour-long episodes and released in two tantalising parts. Surely, this is when we'd finally learn which racist royals had disgracefully smeared their unborn child and who exactly had callously refused Meghan's plea for help at her hour of utmost need? Not a word of it.

The deceit began before the series was even released. Netflix released the first trailers for the series to coincide with a visit by the Prince and Princess of Wales to the US, the first major royal tour since the Queen's death. Any benefit of the doubt about unfortunate coincidences was squashed when self-appointed Meghan publicist Omid Scobie posted: 'If tomorrow is Prince William's Super Bowl, then here's your Halftime Show.' It was a typically grubby, cynical, self-serving ploy to overshadow a crucial restorative moment for William and Kate, whom they have long resented for being more popular and – as the future King and Queen – more important.

Misleading use of carefully selected clips and photographs in the trailer was so egregious that even the BBC weighed in with a story documenting their sleight of hand. One showed a braying pack of paparazzi photographers, jostling for space to hound the happy couple. Childhood photographs of Harry were overlaid to evoke the tragic death of his mother Diana. But the photographers shown were actually at the premiere of a *Harry Potter* movie – five years before the couple met. No royals were even present that day.

An apparently sneaky paparazzo was shown lurking high above the Sussexes to steal a shot of them walking with their baby. But it quickly emerged that he had been invited – *by them* – to document their meeting with Desmond Tutu. Another photo showed Harry stretching out his hand to shield the couple's privacy as flashbulbs illuminated his panic-stricken face. It was cropped to disguise the fact that Harry was hugging his ex-girlfriend Chelsy Davy, way back in 2007 when Meghan Markle was starring as a briefcase girl on the US game show *Deal or No Deal*. A rabid press scrum shown hounding the couple in the street was really outside an entirely unrelated court appearance by British model Katie Price. If the UK media's harassment was so unrelenting and vile, why couldn't they find a single legitimate clip to illustrate it?

The first three hours of the show doubled down on the narrative that a happy couple were hounded out of the racist UK by a bullying press. Reviews were unkind – even the *Guardian* called it 'sickening' – but I knew the publicity meant it would be a global smash hit. I watched with mounting fury as they portrayed my country to the rest of the world as a spiteful bigoted hellhole where the press simply would not tolerate a biracial royal family. The British tabloid press has undeniably behaved badly in the past, mirroring times when society writ large was far less tolerant of minorities of all kinds. But Harry and Meghan got none of that.

Meghan was in fact lauded for bringing diversity and star power to the dated monarchy. Together with William and Kate they were hailed as the fresh-faced 'fab four' who could rejuvenate the royal brand for the twenty-first century.

The wall-to-wall veneration reached its climax at their £32 million wedding as one prominent royal commentator gushed: 'To borrow the words of Dr King, this was a day when little black girls could watch TV and genuinely share little white girls' long-held dreams of one day marrying a Prince.' The author? Piers Morgan.

The Netflix series made relentless distasteful use of Harry's late mother, Princess Diana, to stoke sympathy for Meghan. As a tabloid editor I knew Diana quite well, spoke to her regularly and sometimes had lunch with her. She knew how to use the power of the press when she needed to and was every bit as cunningly smart as she was gloriously charming.

The vain attempt to put Meghan on the same lofty pedestal as the most famous and most pursued royal in history was frankly disgraceful. Princess Diana faced more intrusion on any single day of her adult life than Meghan has in her lifetime. And the whole simpering sob story about star-crossed lovers who fled for the safety and privacy of their young family just doesn't pass muster.

They moved to California, celebrity Mecca, where they immediately signed massive podcast and streaming deals before taking regular public potshots at their estranged family and allowing a documentary crew to film their every move. They don't want privacy; they want propaganda.

The final episodes of their constructed reality show attempted to construct a reality that was recognisable only to Harry and Meghan – torching what little was left of their relationship with the royals. Their lawyer spoke about 'a real war' on Meghan, which felt particularly jarring as Russian missiles pounded maternity hospitals in Ukraine.

Harry mauled his brother William, painting him as a 'screaming' hot head who 'bullied' them out of the family and was complicit in press smears on the Sussexes. He accused his own dad, the King, of being a 'liar' who put vanity before fatherhood. Even the recently deceased Queen was appallingly presented as a dupe, manipulated by sinister courtiers in the dark plot against them. All of it was based on a breathless one-sided account of family conversations that were obviously intended to be, yes, private.

The late Queen's mother used to say the secret to remaining a beloved royal was 'never complain, never explain' and that became the guiding principle of Palace communications for most of the Queen's 70 years on the throne. The family must have been anguished and enraged to stand by as their reputations were trashed on a global platform, but the Palace maintained its usual dignified silence. Netflix opened the show with a disclaimer: 'Members of the Royal Family declined to comment on the content within this series.' To this day their only comment on the documentary has been to categorically deny ever being asked to comment.

Pretty much everybody else in the world had something to say – how could they not? It was a blistering attack not only on the institution of the monarchy but also on the senior royals who represent the UK to the rest of the world. Many people were furious.

Long-serving BBC royal correspondent Nicholas Witchell, normally unruffled and bent double to avoid controversy, said on live TV: 'The idea that anyone was out to destroy her, frankly, I think is absurd and simply does not stand up to proper and reasonable scrutiny.'

Reporters had a field day filleting the show to expose a whole catalogue of fibs, ranging from Meghan's bogus claim that she received 'no training' on how to be a royal and an instantly disproven boast that she always wore muted colours to avoid standing out. The reality was she wore more primary colours than the Pride flag, as hundreds of official photographs proved immediately. Harry was also mocked for insisting he was bravely 'speaking truth to power'. Yes, Prince Henry Charles Albert David, The Duke of Sussex, Earl of Dumbarton and Baron Kilkeel, sticking it to the big guy!

The show was a massive publicity success and remains one of the biggest series ever on Netflix. They very savvily manipulated the clickbait culture of social media valida-tion, which rewards victimhood without evidence and wallowing without reason. But at what cost? They had sold their royal souls to become reality stars. They severed

their link to the one thing that made them interesting –
royalty. And as they are now discovering, it was a Faustian
pact. You can only do that once.

They now have to rely on their subatomic nano-person-
alities, which is proving to be exactly as fruitful as I'd
expect. There has been a much broader cultural backlash
to the trend of automatically exalting every self-
proclaimed victim of anything. Too many innocent
bystanders were caught in the MeToo and BLM nets. Too
many boys cried wolf. Suddenly personal injustice warriors are regarded with at least a bit of scepticism until they
show the one thing Harry and Meghan have never
provided – proof.

Harry's memoir *Spare* was one last dip in the royal reve-
lations river as it rapidly ran dry. The 416-page self-helpless
book detailed every grievance he'd ever had while trading
his dignity for a reported $27 million fee. The privacy-
obsessed prince laid bare every tawdry detail of his previously private life, from drug abuse to losing his virginity
and getting frostbite on his 'todger' after a trip to the
North Pole.

Having wailed about his security – even suing the
British state for downgrading his taxpayer-funded protections – he chose to boast about killing 25 Taliban 'chess
pieces' as a soldier in Afghanistan. This crass misjudgement was criticised by even those who served alongside
him, given that it risked endangering both them and the
security teams who currently look after him. And he again
spared no mercy for his closest family, accusing brother
William of knocking him down in a physical attack and

branding stepmother Camilla a 'dangerous villain' who sacrificed him at 'her personal PR altar'. Rest in peace, irony.

Most outrageously of all, Harry's promotional media tour included a primetime interview with ITV in which he dramatically and ludicrously washed his hands of the original race charge against the royals. 'In the Oprah interview, you accuse members of your family of racism,' Tom Bradby said, correctly.

'No,' Harry snapped, before clarifying: 'Racism and unconscious bias, the two things are different.' What in the yellow-bellied HR committee psychobabble was he talking about? They literally flew to New York – on a private jet, obviously – to collect a human rights award for their 'heroic' stand against 'structural racism'.

The impact of those Oprah race claims was tectonic. Tens of millions of people around the world were left with the unavoidable impression that Britain is a racist country, with racists at the very heart of our royal family.

A stony-faced Don Lemon, who (formerly) made a living hawking his divisive 'us vs them' takes on US TV, told CNN viewers: 'The whole institution is built on a racist structure ... of course they are racist! That's what the entire monarchy is built on.'

Black studies professor Kehinde Andrews, whose greatest hits include the outrageous claim that the British Empire was worse than Hitler's Nazis, thundered: 'Blackness and the monarchy are like oil and water.' He concluded that the only feasible way to cleanse the monarchy of its racism curse was total and immediate abolition.

Global media duly began scouring every royal outing for a subtle sign of simmering internal bigotry. A Caribbean tour by the Cambridges, which would normally have fluttered by as a medley of smiley photo opportunities, was engulfed by a contrived debate about past imperial sins. Professor Andrews leaped into action again, deriding a disastrous 'colonial nostalgia tour' and ordering remittances of £7.5 *trillion* to former colonies for 'unpaid labour and traumatic damages'.

Every subsequent royal tour and Commonwealth summit has been overshadowed by arguments about reparations, demands for apologies and self-flagellating about learning the lessons of the past. No wonder Harry, who has in fact built quite a nice life atop these 'structurally racist foundations', decided to dial it down a bit.

Britain's monarchy undoubtedly has a lot to answer for, if you consider the grand sweep of history. Henry VIII had what's now known as a 'problematic' relationship with women, especially when they were in close proximity to a bladed weapon. His daughter Queen Mary enjoyed burning Protestants in front of large crowds, which is almost certainly now a 'hate crime'. Britain has had kings and queens for 1,200 years, so it stands to reason that some have been dumb, mean, malevolent or useless. But it would be quite odd for King Charles to apologise for historic misogyny because James VI hunted old ladies he suspected of being witches.

The British Empire did some very good things and some very evil things. It brought the benefits of contemporary civilisation to hundreds of millions of people – roads, railways, schools and common law. It created the trading routes from which the modern global economy emerged. It educated millions of people. But it also plundered indigenous resources and violently squashed many acts of rebellion.

Most shamefully of all, it shipped 3 million African people to the Americas as slaves. Portugal and Spain actually began the slave trade – one of the great stains on humanity – Britain and France then industrialised the suffering. Nations like Denmark, the Dutch Republic and Sweden were culpable too, as were the African leaders who disgustingly caged their own people for profit. Britain eventually outlawed the transatlantic slave trade and sent the Royal Navy to suppress it. About 2,000 naval men died trying.

History is ugly, complicated and riddled with heinous deeds committed in less enlightened times. None of it has anything much to do with King Charles III – or you, or me. If modern royals have to apologise for slavery, surely they should also therefore be graciously thanked for ending it? Both ideas are ridiculous and divisive. As with the debate about reparations in the US, it makes regular people who had nothing at all to do with historic slavery feel they're under attack for something they detest as much as everybody else. And where does it all stop?

Do I get reparations from Italy for the carnage wrought on Britain by invading Romans? I'll also be asking for big cheques from Denmark, Norway and Sweden on account of the marauding Vikings, who exuberantly enslaved ancient Brits after pillaging our towns and villages. If the

UK government forked out £7.5 trillion to the distant descendants of people who actually did suffer, as Kehinde Andrews demands, it would bankrupt the country. Future generations in Barbados would have to pay reparations to Britain for the misery caused by the British reparations.

They rode the coat-tails of the mobs toppling sinful statues; at a moment when Making America Great Again was a polarising ambition and Greta Thunberg had convinced throngs of young people that their own relatively friendly nations were somehow worse than China or Russia. It never made sense. For centuries, both the US and UK have remained among the most desirable nations on earth for migrants. They don't come because we're racist. They come because, by every available metric, we are tolerant, welcoming and great.

Patriotism is back in business after this period of intense browbeating – and trade is roaring. It's very difficult to look at the atrocities between Israel and Hamas or the misery in Ukraine and maintain the illusion that *we* are the bad guys. Or that our social squabbles are the real problem. Mostly people just got sick of being told to apologise for loathsome traits they simply did not recognise in themselves.

Ironically, the monarchy that Harry and Meghan trashed has always been a vessel for a healthy, unifying type of patriotism that is unsullied by politics. Big royal occasions, like the King's coronation, bring everybody together in celebration of how we all ended up here together. The royals may bitterly disappoint us (cc: Prince Andrew) but we still love the institution, just as families stick with football teams for generations even when the current players are garbage.

There's no doubt the royals felt personally wounded by the attacks, not least with regard to racism. Even the late Queen – the grand dame of 'never complain, never explain' – responded to the Oprah claims. Her legendarily laconic dismissal was a masterclass in understated withering: 'Recollections may vary.' Prince William felt compelled to break protocol to tell reporters: 'We are very much not a racist family.' I gladly played a small role in burying the obscene race claims for good.

Omid Scobie published a gossipy, pro-Sussex book called *Endgame* in 2023. Meghan famously denied briefing him for his first book – before apologising in court and admitting that, obviously, she had. He boasted that he knew the names of Meghan's 'royal racists' – he has impeccable sources, as we know – and simply couldn't use them for legal reasons. But the names appeared in the Dutch edition of *Endgame*. After some robust debate with my bosses at the time, I named them live on air as King Charles and Catherine, Princess of Wales.

I did that for several reasons. First, speculation was raging out of control, dragging the whole royal family across the coals again. Second, it made no sense that Dutch journalists and readers knew the names but British people didn't. Third, once you know the names at the centre of the whole multi-year firestorm, it becomes blindingly obvious just how absurd the accusations are. Whatever your view of the monarchy, I don't think any serious person really believes that King Charles or the

Princess of Wales have a racist bone in their bodies. Judging by the public reaction, this was only the endgame for the royal race-baiters.

Both the King and Princess of Wales revealed they were battling cancer in early 2024 in two bombshell announcements that came just weeks apart. Both were met with an outpouring of public sympathy. They won plaudits worldwide for sharing the grim news and emboldening others to do the same. They didn't get everything right, of course. The insatiable hunger for constant bulletins sparked outlandish speculation about Kate in particular, and a disastrously edited Mother's Day photo fuelled rampant conspiracy theories online. But they very quickly put that right.

A few months before she got the all-clear, the Prince and Princess of Wales released a stunningly powerful three-minute film about Kate's battle with cancer to reveal she'd now completed chemotherapy. In decades of royal coverage, I had never seen anything like it. Soul-stirring footage showed the family and their children embracing and holding hands; clearly besotted with one another. Kate's commentary about her personal health struggle and the impact on her family was word-perfect in its honesty, humility and hope.

Little more than an hour later, Netflix released a promo for a new series on polo made by Harry and Meghan. One video was an extraordinarily powerful, moving and profoundly inspiring insight into what it's like to have a life-threatening illness when you have a loving young family, irrespective of wealth or status. The other, featuring two brats who ditched royal duty and service for self-enriching Hollywood glamour, was a self-promotional plug for a series on a sport so elite that only millionaires play it.

Regardless of whether Meghan and Harry deliberately rushed out this promo to spoil Kate's announcement, or just to capitalise on the megaton-sized global attention it instantly received, it landed like a plop of pigeon poop on a bare head. The same can be said of everything they've done since. *Polo* was scorched by critics and watched by almost nobody. Spotify abruptly cancelled its $20 million deal with the Sussexes, which yielded just 12 episodes in two years of a show called *Archetypes*. Bill Simmons, Spotify's head of talk strategy, felt they got the name wrong: 'The *Fucking Grifters*,' he reflected. 'That's the podcast we should have launched with them.' Meghan's Netflix lifestyle show – *With Love, Meghan* – was derided as 'toe-curlingly unlovable' by the *Guardian* and quickly followed *Polo* into the ratings abyss.

The show was supposed to take fans behind the curtain of their California home for an intimate insight into Meghan's post-royal life as she chatted with friends and shared tips on cooking, gardening and – bizarrely – transferring supermarket pretzels from one plastic bag to another unbranded plastic bag. But it's really one big vanity project and a glossy ad for her new range of jam. It wasn't even filmed in their home – just a rented mansion that 'echoes their own space'. The brutal truth is that nobody cares about their post-royal life.

I've long called for King Charles to remove their royal titles and cut off their only remaining monetisable feature.

One of her celebrity friends in the show, Mindy Kaling, is admonished for referring to Meghan by her surname Markle. Meghan butts in: 'It's so funny that you keep saying Meghan Markle, you know I'm Sussex now?' That's not even how it works. The family name she married into is Windsor. The title of Sussex, which happens to be my home county, was awarded to them by the monarchy they abandoned and she has reportedly spent less than six hours there in her entire life.

I'm very often accused of being 'obsessed' with Harry and Meghan, but the truth is I find them increasingly tedious. I comment on them, as everybody else does, because they keep doing outrageous things. Every point I've made here is deliberately illustrated with commentary from others in the media, which is not difficult to find.

They are extremely wealthy celebrities who perform for the media circus to fund their lifestyles. I'm paid to give my opinions on things and every metric indicates that people are interested in what I have to say about them. That is partly because Meghan's failed attempt to defenestrate me has made me a small storyline in the soap opera they crafted to settle scores and sell their wares. I truly relish the day they are so irrelevant I don't have to talk about them any more, and it appears to be almost upon us.

Fighting their claims has never been about arguing that racism doesn't exist – or even that no royals have ever been racist. The common-sense backlash is to a divisive doctrine that says everybody is racist, consciously or otherwise, and that whole organisations are racist because of bad things that happened centuries ago.

At first glance, the British monarchy should be finished. How can a definitionally elitist system of illogical birth-rights survive in a society that loathes 'privilege' and rages against 'elites'? It prevails precisely because it stands for nothing but continuity in a world roiled by people who want to change everything. It has survived woke, and survived the Sussexes, the way it inexorably survives every crisis.

Harry and Meghan threw the kitchen sink at mobilising culture warriors for their crusade. There was victimhood, trauma, mental health, social justice, racial justice, person-alised truth. But most people are sick of all that – and of them. Ultimately the public looked at the battle fought by two distressed virtuous damsels amid a great virtuous social reckoning and they still sided with the aristocratic symbol of apparent colonial wickedness. As I said, woke is dead.

Chapter 13

HOLLYWOOD HYPOCRISY

*Never let facts get in the way of a good story,
especially if it's one about how the world would be
so much better without all the men in it.*

Snow White and the Seven Dwarfs is one of the most
beloved movies in cinematic history. The original Disney
animation, based on a fairytale that has enchanted children for two hundred years, made more than two billion
dollars in today's money. Almost everybody has seen it and
almost everybody loves it. A glossy $270 million remake
should have been smooth sailing, followed by a walk in
the park and a quick round of shooting fish in a barrel.
Instead it's one of the most catastrophic face-planting flops
of all time – and movies may never be the same again.

Hollywood has long been at the vanguard of the most
tone-deaf brand of wokery. Pampered stars file into the
Oscars, wearing gowns and jewels worth millions, before
pontificating on stage about social justice and the various
moral crusades of the moment. They live in an impenetra-

ble bubble of hypocrisy, inside which it somehow makes perfect sense to laud feminism and the MeToo movement while handing awards and ovations to fugitive paedophile Roman Polanski. We indulge them because they're beautiful, they're talented and they entertain us with great movies. That's the deal. But they're no longer keeping their end of the bargain.

Movies have become moralising bilge. Entertainment is now a secondary concern to the core mission of making you feel like a terrible person. Hollywood executives have whipped themselves into a frenzy of self-importance and run wild with the idea that tokenistic casting and homiletic storylines will mean we, too, become woke. But audiences can no longer be taken for granted.

I can find any movie or series ever made without leaving the house. Why would I buy tickets for a turgid, virtuous sermon that makes me want to sit on my TV and watch the armchair? Inevitably, this bubble has now spectacularly burst and the calamitous *Snow White* remake jabbed in the pin. It is the definitive masterclass in 'go woke, go broke' and should be taught in future history classes on how society revolted against cultural insanity.

The unravelling began before a single frame was filmed. In 2022, the US was still grappling with its grand 'racial reckoning', the post-BLM over-correction that made whiteness an irrevocable cultural sin. This was bad news for Snow White, who was named after her 'skin white as snow' in the original fairytale.

Not to be accused of failing to 'meet the moment', Disney announced the new live action *Snow White* would star Hispanic actress Rachel Zegler. There's nothing like a Latina Snow White to shatter the glass ceiling that shamefully denies billions of women their right to play extremely pale princesses in massive Hollywood productions.

I don't find a Latina Snow White to be at all problematic, but the hypocrisy is insightful. There are no diversity quotas in Disney's *Black Panther* or *Mulan*, for example, nor should we expect them. And in recent years we've been repeatedly lectured about how plum roles should be awarded only to actors whose appearance, ethnicity and sexual preferences closely track those of the fictional character.

Scarlett Johansson was slammed for taking a role based on a Japanese animation, even though she is neither Asian nor a cartoon. Eddie Redmayne was bullied into a grovelling public apology for portraying a trans woman in *The Danish Girl*. A 'Jewface' scandal erupted when gentile Bradley Cooper played Leonard Bernstein in a big budget biopic. And Bryan Cranston faced a backlash for his starring role as a disabled millionaire in *The Upside*. His withering response was word perfect: 'It's called acting!'

Zegler's main issue, however, is not that she's Latina. Nor is it that she lacks talent, which as a singer and performer she has in spades. It's simply that she's outrageously obnoxious. In the very first press interviews, she began hammering the cherished original movie with a man-bashing mallet.

'It is no longer 1937,' she revealed exclusively for the cameras, '[Snow White] is not going to be saved by the prince. She's not going to be dreaming about true love.

She's dreaming about becoming the leader she knows she can be.' First, what's wrong with doing both? And does every little girl really have to dream of becoming the Head of Accounting or Hillary Clinton? This was the first clue that Disney would be ticking the 'strong woman' box among others on its very long fun-destroying checklist.

Zegler provided the confirmation of Disney's intentions when she derided the original fairytale prince as 'creepy and stalker-ish' in a lazy sop to MeToo empowerment. Lest we forget that the prince's allegedly predatory conduct was giving Snow White a kiss to lift her from a poison apple-induced eternal coma, which sounds like the right thing to do. This is now a recurring trope in Hollywood. Movie studios have collectively decided that amplifying strong female leads is not enough on its own. The message will only really hit home if it's accompanied by the humiliation or total erasure of all men.

A disastrous 2016 remake of *Ghostbusters* features an all-female ghoul-removal team who recruit Chris Hemsworth as a dim-witted male secretary based only on his looks. *Ocean's 8* replaced George Clooney's gang of suave superthieves with a gaggle of strong independent female heisters while every man in the movie is evil or an idiot. Amazon's *Rings of Power* over promoted all the secondary female characters while – according to *The Lord of the Rings* superfan Elon Musk – 'every male character ... is a coward, a jerk or both'. Besides this brazen misandry, what all of these massively expensive remakes have in common is that they were a critical and box office disaster.

Greta Gerwig's *Barbie* bucked this trend at the box office but was rendered unwatchable by running amok with the same man-throttling message. The word 'patriarchy' is used endlessly in the movie – even though most people have no idea what it means. Barbie lives in Barbie World alongside many diverse Barbies – including a trans Barbie, a disabled Barbie and a black female president Barbie.

The Barbies are all-powerful while the Kens are all useless second-class halfwits. Mattel, which owns the Barbie brand, is depicted as a misogynistic bearpit with an all-male board of alpha dogs, even though Barbie was invented by a woman and the real-life Mattel has many women on its board. Never let facts get in the way of a good story, especially if it's one about how the world would be so much better without all the men in it.

Without spoiling all of the movie – the plot does that for itself – Ken returns from a trip to the misogynistic real world filled with toxic male malice. The blameless Barbies unite to defeat the moronic Kens in a giant battle of the sexes, who are restored to their role as subservient halfwits. I always assumed it wasn't 'equality' if one side gets annihilated.

The real world I live in is full of confident, high-achieving women who scoff at such derisory misrepresentation of their lowly status. And if anybody made a movie that ridicules women as much as Barbie loathes men, they wouldn't just be cancelled, they'd be strung up in the town square and pelted with rotten vegetables.

Barbie may have been extremely irritating, but millions of people paid to see it before forming an opinion. The loathing for Disney's all-new *Snow White* was all pre-emptive; propelled by a succession of spectacular own goals.

Controversy reached boiling point when photos of the production and set were leaked to the *Daily Mail*. The illicit snaps revealed a sizeable problem. The dwarfs were gone. Banished! And not by the Wicked Queen. They had bitten the poisoned apple of diversity and inclusion. Grumpy, Sleepy, Dopey and the whole gang of diminutive guardians had been replaced by seven 'diverse magical creatures' of varying genders, races and heights. Surely some mistake? Disney first insisted the characters were fake, which is a difficult line to maintain when you intend to release a movie with them in it, before eventually admitting they were merely 'unofficial'. And the studio confirmed it was taking a 'different approach' to the dwarfs.

This novel new approach to dwarfs turned out to be abolishing them altogether. Disney's explanation for doing so became an instant classic in the canon of woke self-cannibalism. The studio soberly announced that it would not be casting any dwarfs as the dwarfs to 'avoid reinforcing stereotypes from the original animated film'.

Excuse me? Which harmful stereotypes were they afraid of perpetuating? The dwarfs are the heroes of the whole story! Not only do they shelter the stricken princess in their charming home and cater for her every whim, they chase the Wicked Queen off the end of a cliff after a high-speed chase in a thunderstorm. *Snow White* without the seven dwarfs is like remaking *Top Gun* with no aeroplanes to reduce their carbon footprint. It's ludicrous. The only conceivable stereotype in *Snow White* is that dwarfs are small – which they are – and if Disney thinks that's a problem I'd say *they* are the dwarfists.

Game of Thrones star Peter Dinklage, the world's most famous and successful dwarf actor, had terrified Hollywood executives with an expletive-laden rant about their failure to cast dwarfs in serious roles. 'They were very proud to cast a Latina actress as Snow White,' he said on a podcast. 'You're progressive in one way but you're still making that fucking backward story of seven dwarfs living in the cave. What the fuck are you doing, man?'

Dinklage is a great actor and I completely agree that dwarfs should be able to play all sorts of characters. But the seven dwarfs didn't live in a cave: it was a cosy, story-book cottage in the woods with hand-crafted furniture and a roaring fire. And Dinklage had unwittingly given progressives another minority cause to, ironically, chase off the edge of a cliff.

Disney's attempt at inclusion had led to the *exclusion* of dwarf actors from the one big budget movie that could have employed a whole squad of them. Self-professed wokie and cultural commentator James Barr attempted a defence of their position on *Uncensored*.

'They shouldn't be called dwarfs,' he said, fumbling desperately for reasons why the original cartoon could in any way be described as inappropriate. Unfortunately for Barr, I had also invited dwarf actor Dylan Postl, a former WWE star, who appeared on the big screen to call him out: 'I would love to hear – what *should* I call myself, sir?' James looked increasingly like he wanted to disappear into a very large hole as Dylan perfectly articulated why the moral crusaders had become tangled in their own net.

'There are dwarf actors that dream to be in a major motion picture such as this Disney remake,' he said. 'Now it's taken away because of, quote unquote, "progression" and all that. It's not right.' Dylan pointed out that Peter Dinklage had already found vast fame and fortune – by playing an *imp* – and had thrown his less famous peers under a virtue-signalling bus.

'I can't go out for the Harrison Ford or George Clooney roles,' Dylan said, correctly. 'These dwarf roles are for people of *my* stature.' Disney was forced to respond to the furore by reinstating the dwarfs – but only as nightmarish animated CGI creatures that looked like evil garden gnomes. An official trailer revealing the badly drawn beasts became the most 'disliked' movie trailer in YouTube history.

Star Rachel Zegler put the final nail in *Snow White's* coffin in the build-up to the premiere, using Instagram to announce that she was 'speechless' about Donald Trump's election victory. Unfortunately for Disney's executives and accountants, she was not. Zegler raged that she hoped 'Trump supporters and Trump voters and Trump himself may never know peace'. Her decision to trash a majority of the voting public doubtless contributed to a box office catastrophe, with endless viral clips of empty theatres and a net loss of more than $100 million.

One rogue dud is forgivable but *Snow White* was really the final act in a multi-year campaign of indoctrination by a company that has totally abandoned its role of merely entertaining children and families. Leaked videos revealed executive producer Latoya Raveneau, a proud 'biromantic asexual' (me neither), boasting about a 'not-at-all-secret gay agenda' and 'wherever I could, adding queerness'.

Toy Story spin-off *Lightyear* duly featured a lesbian kiss, prompting a boycott from conservative parents and another loss of $100 million. Director Taika Waititi crowed about making his *Thor* movie 'super-gay'. Disney's animated *Baymax!* series featured a burly trans character buying sanitary pads. Honestly, who wants to watch that? It's all just so exhausting.

Almost 15 years ago the Stonewall LGBT charity ran a massive billboard campaign with big posters reading: 'Some People Are Gay. Get Over It!' That's exactly how I feel. Why can't we go back to *that* era of rainbow activism? I really don't care what you do in your own bedroom. And I felt that way long before they made a gay *Toy Story*.

As well as packing identity politics into its fictitious storylines, Disney has also begun dabbling in real politics. The company publicly condemned a bill from Florida's governor Ron DeSantis to ban schools from teaching gender ideology to children in primary-grade levels, even as polls showed most parents supported it.

Staff had staged a walkout calling on CEO Bob Chapek to speak out and he promptly caved with a statement condemning the bill as a 'challenge to basic human rights'. The company has no comment about doing business in many countries where homosexuality is fully illegal. Nor did it criticise authorities in Xinjiang, where it shamefully filmed its *Mulan* remake within spitting distance of Uighur internment camps.

The studio announced with great fanfare in 2022 that 50 per cent of all of its characters would now be either LGBTQIA or from other 'underrepresented groups'. Clearly, this courtesy did not extend to dwarfs! Netflix has also made such a habit of casting black actors as white historical figures that it is now mercilessly parodied online, with social media users mocking up movie posters like '*Zelensky* – starring Idris Elba'.

Disney inevitably took it a step further, crowbarring heavy-handed racial messaging into shows for children. A jaw-dropping episode of *The Proud Family* went viral for featuring children demanding reparations and singing about 'white supremacy' in a Black Lives Matter-inspired tirade about slavery. This is divisive trash. It's teaching kids to hate each other. Parents should be able to sit their children in front of the TV without fearing they'll be force-fed extremist propaganda based on the ultra-woke worldview of a few Hollywood executives.

I have never seen any of the *Star Wars* movies and have no interest in little frogs waving neon bulbs around. So when Mark Hamill appeared on *Uncensored* shortly after complaining that he only gets asked about *Star Wars* in his TV interviews, I revealed I'd never seen it. He didn't really seem to like that, either.

Those who do follow the franchise reliably inform me that it has been thoroughly woke-washed in Disney's hands, with stars backing a 'The Force is Female' campaign and a massive diversity drive, which satisfied nobody. Lucasfilm's president Kathleen Kennedy, who oversaw the diverse new *Star Wars*, was superbly satirised by the caustic cartoon *South Park*. It depicted her as showing her turning up on various film sets to bellow 'put a chick in it and make her gay!' That does seem to be the formula – but it's not winning.

None of this makes me want to dash off down to the movies and I'm clearly not alone. Cinemas have still not recovered from their pandemic slump. Disney lost a fortune on a succession of high-profile bombs and even its superhero hit factory has run out of steam. *The Marvels*, starring Brie Larson as a typical Hollywood girlboss who regards men with profound disgust, lost an eyewatering $237 million.

The movie had been criticised by some fans for its diverse and female-led cast, prompting director Nia DaCosta to lambast them as 'violent and racist and sexist and homophobic and all of those awful things'. Is it any wonder they didn't turn up? British actor John Boyega, who appears in three *Star Wars* movies, similarly slammed its fans as bigots and called it 'the most whitest, elite space'. Audiences are clearly sick of paying to see hectoring and high-minded stories made by people who hate them. It doesn't have to be this way.

The long-awaited sequel to *Top Gun* raked in $1.4 billion and became the biggest hit of Tom Cruise's stellar Hollywood career. It's a jet-fuelled, balls-out, supersonic rampage with cocksure men who drink, fight, defy orders, ride motorbikes without helmets, bond over fixing engines, bottle up their feelings, bail out their buddies, bed the hot girls and kill the bad guys. I went to see it with two of my sons and it was the best escapist fun I've had at the movies since 1986, when a 21-year-old Piers went to see the original *Top Gun* movie at the cinema – ten times.

Maverick is pure entertainment. No politics. No preaching. No moralising. No 'message'. We don't even really know who the bad guys are and we don't really care because we won and they're dead. The movie jetted directly into all the swirls of gloom about toxic masculinity and hit them with a Massive Ordnance Penetrator, to quote the amusingly phallic-sounding weapon used by the US to hit Iran's nuclear sites.

Not everybody agrees, of course. I interviewed legendary Oscar-winner Micky Rourke for *Uncensored* not long after the movie came out. 'That don't mean shit to me,' he said of *Maverick's* record-breaking receipts. '[Tom Cruise] has been doing the same effing part for 35 years. I got no respect for that.' Ouch! Rourke actually turned down the role of Iceman in the original *Top Gun*, paving the way for the masterful Val Kilmer. His incredibly poignant appearance in the sequel – persuaded by close friend Tom Cruise to return despite his very grave illness – almost brought a tear to my eye in the cinema.

The main reason I love both *Top Gun* movies so much is that I came out of the cinema feeling better than when I walked in. Surely, that's the whole point? I'm not some turtleneck-wearing movie critic or savant. Like the vast majority of the paying public, I just want to be entertained. I'd rather not be force-fed kale when I'm trying to eat popcorn. But the onslaught has been relentless. And the po-faced execs who wreck modern movies have been busily discovering ways of invading the old ones, too.

Disney has been criticised for slapping trigger warnings at the beginning of its classics like *Dumbo, Peter Pan* and *The Aristocats* to warn of horrors to come. 'This programme includes negative depictions or mistreatment of people or cultures,' it laments. 'These stereotypes were wrong then and are wrong now.' It's like saying 'enjoy the show everybody – but please make sure you feel really bloody awful about it.' Mercifully, Disney is preparing to downplay the content warnings on its streaming service. Has anybody really ever been radicalised as a racist by a flying cartoon elephant?

The British Film Institute added trigger warnings to a couple of old James Bond movies, which cautioned about 'language, images or other content that reflect views prevalent in its time, but will cause offence today'. Offence to who exactly? Academics have actually found that anybody with genuine trauma is more likely to be upset *by* a trigger warning because it makes them think of the one thing they didn't want to think about. It can't be long before movies start with a trigger warning that says: 'Warning! We are about to show you a trigger warning.'

James Bond is, of course, another victim of this uncultural revolution. The great 007 has been ritually emasculated for the MeToo era, with papoose-wearing Daniel Craig playing him as an emotional wreck who wants to sit and talk to women about his feelings instead of sleeping with them. Craig boasted about being more naked in his movies than the Bond girls, while producer Barbara Broccoli marvelled that Bond is now 'allowed to be vulnerable'.

Sorry but no, he's not. This is quite simple. James Bond is a steely-eyed, debonair dealer of shagging and death. For two or three hours, every two or three years, we pay to be enthralled by his fictitious world of assassins, gadgets and supervillains. It's supposed to be a distraction from our everyday drudgery and quarrelling, not an extension of it.

Hollywood is now finally waking up. Just like the proverbial tree falling in a deserted forest, there are no movies without audiences who want to watch them. Disney quietly cut a trans-themed episode from a new *Marvel* show and said it will remove a transgender storyline from a new Pixar series because it realises parents prefer to discuss these issues – or not – independently.

Big studios are hurriedly reviewing their upcoming movies to scrub out any ammunition for a *Snow White*-style recoil. Releases like *American Fiction* and The Daily Wire documentary *Am I Racist?* found traction in cinemas by making woke the butt of the joke. This is great news for anybody who thinks films and cinema are supposed to be enjoyable. I want the next 007 movie to open with the eponymous assassin taking a massive, defiant swig of his martini and announcing: 'My pronouns are Bond, James Bond.'

PART FOUR
THE COMMON-SENSE REVOLUTION

Woke is dead. The mourning period will be so brief you might actually have already missed it. Champagne is flowing at the wake and everybody is relieved to finally admit they really couldn't stand it all in the first place. But we're not totally in the clear. The celebrations will be short-lived too unless we collectively take a big sniff of the smelling salts and learn the tough lessons of a rough few years that have only made us more anxious, hostile and miserable.

Chapter 14

LISTEN TO YOUR INNER VOICE

The next moralistic movement will have some scary
new weapons in its armoury and needs to be met by
a wall of very human gut instincts.

I thoroughly enjoy both winning arguments and saying 'I told you so,' but that wasn't the point of the fight against woke. It's not about avenging enemies or being right but creating a saner world for the next generation with less tribalism, less intransigence, less division and more tolerance for ideas we don't instinctively share. That is probably what woke intended to do. But 'inclusive' only included the people who agreed. Everybody else had to be crushed. And the aimless conflict of it all is a big part of why it failed.

Big movements for social change always come and go, but they usually have more to show for their efforts at the end of it. The progressive era in the early 1900s was a fight for fair wages, women's suffrage, outlawing child labour and rooting out political corruption. The civil rights movement hammered a path to the end of racial discrimination and segregation. The countercultural hippies spread an intoxicating (and intoxicated) message of individual freedom and a revulsion to violent death and war. They were influential, impactful and often popular because they were grounded in changes for the better that most people felt good about.

That same spirit of positive change is why the big censorship campaigns of the twentieth century were all repelled. They came from conservatives back then; railing against 'smut', comic books, glossy magazines and art. In 1990, a museum director in Cincinnati was prosecuted for hosting an exhibition of Robert Mapplethorpe's photographs, some of which are lewd and decidedly 'challenging', in what's now known as the Mapplethorpe Obscenity Trial. A jury took just minutes to side with the waves of protesters who defended the right to expression and personal choice. A rural tractor driver who'd never been to an art gallery travelled for hours to see the exhibition, incensed at being told he wasn't allowed to see something if he chose to.

Woke, on the other hand, is fundamentally negative, accusatory and dismal. 'Peace and love' and 'I have a dream' became 'check your privilege' and 'silence is violence'. There's no trace of the warm and fuzzy idea that we can all play a part in making the world a better place. Instead everybody is drafted for war based on their race or sexual preferences and sent into an endless battle with sinister hidden forces and each other.

It's not really *for* anything in particular, like paid holidays or women's right to vote, but *against* everybody who refuses to conform. The civil rights activists won racial equality in law. The hippies helped turn Americans and the world against the disastrous war in Vietnam. Gay men and women won the right to marry and then proudly celebrate their unions at a month-long rainbow party we all have to attend, every single year.

Wokies haven't achieved anything of lasting relevance because they didn't really try to. The main aim was always to shame and vilify the imaginary privileged oppressors, who were basically anybody who wasn't as perfect as they think they are. Their gluttonous demand for shocking grievances always exceeded the actual supply. That's why there has been so much outrage over so little and why so many perfectly clear-minded regular people have been caught in the cancellation crosshairs.

A lady who stacked shelves at a British supermarket for 28 years was fired during the BLM riots for jokingly asking whether they should still sell cuddly toys of Bing Bunny, a cartoon black rabbit. A council worker in the north of England was dismissed for putting 'XYchromosomeGuy/ AdultHumanMale' in his email signature instead of his pronouns, even though both declarations achieved the same pointless goal of confirming his instantly self-explanatory gender. A gas worker in California was fired after being filmed making a 'white power' gesture out of his car window, triggering a social media pile-on. It turned out he was a Mexican Latino who had been cracking his knuckles at a traffic light.

A young man at Oxford University tragically took his own life after peers at the college brought the strictures of social media and celebrity cancel culture into the real world. An unproven and relatively trivial claim about an uncomfortable sexual encounter led to what the coroner called a 'self-policing' rush to judgement with 'exclusion and rejection'. The college's inquiries uncovered a 'concerning practice of social ostracism among students, often referred to as a cancel culture'.

I don't think anybody really wants to live in a society of curtain-twitching snitches and armchair detectives raking over 'problematic' social media posts from a decade ago. I don't think anybody really enjoys walking on eggshells and waiting for a knock on the door from the fun police. We've been liberated from the tyranny of the always offended and given a fresh crack at a world without cancel culture. And that's why it's so important that we don't replace it with something equally bitter, ideological, grievance-ridden and censorious.

There isn't really any such thing as an 'anti-woke movement'. I see it more as the inevitable triumph of common-sense ideas that most of us share against radical lunacy, which flourished by pretending to be nice. But if there is a common-sense brigade, and we are all in it, we need to be equally sceptical about daft ideas from people who say they aren't woke at all.

It's nothing much to do with politics. The left wing surrendered in fear to noisy woke lunatics and allowed right-wing populists to dominate the common-sense middle ground, but the next wave of insanity might well come from rabid right-wing headbangers who also have no goals besides wrecking everything to start all over again. Attacks on common sense can spring from the places you least expect to find them, as the woke movement proved.

Almost everybody in my generation agreed with the happy liberal consensus that sprang from the civil rights movement; the idea that all forms of discrimination based on unchangeable characteristics were unacceptable and wrong. But it ended up being the so-called liberals who overturned that applecart by demanding reverse discrimination to settle the scores of the past and trampling free speech to get their way.

We're now seeing the first early murmurings of a new brand of silliness from right-wing people who have spent years railing against all things woke. They have very different opinions about the world but use the woke tactical playbook to win arguments and get what they want. You don't have to travel far on social media before you encounter a furious 'straight white Christian man' who's convinced the whole world is against him.

Straight White Christian Man had many very valid reasons to feel assailed by wokery, but the point is nobody is buying it any more. He can safely come out of his bunker. The last flagbearers of wokery, wandering punch-drunk around the desolate battlefield, are the subject of ridicule not revolution. There's no need to wallow in identity-based victimhood in the same way they did. And your skin pigment and sexuality should not be the most interesting things about you. It's exactly the mindset we've been complaining about.

Imagine there was no backlash to woke and it had bloomed unabated in the most ludicrous ways

241

possible. Imagine J. K. Rowling declaring that men can become women, President Kamala Harris paying out billions in racial reparations and a 60-year-old Michelle Tyson becoming the greatest female boxer of all time.

Fast-forward a few centuries and big companies would be hiring only white men to arrest their social and economic decline. Universities might be run entirely by straight people who believe that straightness has been oppressed by LGBT oppressors. Gay speakers would be hounded off campus by livid protesters. Radical Christian minorities may be allowed to stone adulterers because stopping them would be Christophobic. If all that sounds terrifying and ridiculous – and it's supposed to – it shows how preposterous and damaging identity politics is, no matter which side it comes from.

Konstantin Kisin, who co-hosts the *TRIGGERnometry* podcast, talks about the new phenomenon of the 'woke right' and points out that it shares many of the tools in the woke toolbox that I've laid out in this book. They include: 'deranged worldview … disregard for truth, hatred of The West and falsification of history'. He makes an interesting point.

It's now becoming weirdly fashionable among right-wingers to say things like 'The West has fallen', which they explain by presenting contradictory 'evidence' about the apparent flourishing of Islamic Sharia law and a simultaneous uprising of immoral women who dream only of becoming OnlyFans pornstars. Self-evidently, both of these things can't possibly be true at the same time. It's just another way of sulking about how their own preferred cultural values are not completely dominant.

Conservative megastar Tucker Carlson grilled me in an interview on his show about Britain's triumph against the Nazis in World War II, which I'd always thought was an undisputed success. 'How did you win?' he asked me repeatedly, in his inimitable manic style. 'Is that what victory looks like? You lose all your rights, your economy gets destroyed, you're controlled by bankers and, all of a sudden, oh I won!' As I calmly said to Tucker at the time, we won because I'm not conducting the interview in German with a Nazi boot planted firmly on my neck.

The West has enough problems to fill a whole book of its own, and the decline of traditional Western values is unquestionably a problem, but by every imaginable metric it's still the best place anywhere on earth to be born if you're interested in wealth, healthcare, education, the rule of law, freedom of speech, freedom of faith and living until you're old. I didn't buy the woke woe-is-me idea that everything is so degenerate and awful that we need to smash it up and start again, and I don't buy it from the other side either.

I hosted a debate on *Uncensored* about amateur historian Darryl Cooper, a popular podcaster who makes hugely detailed shows on historical events that are full of wild revisionism. He did a big viral interview with Carlson which included the claim that Sir Winston Churchill was the 'chief villain' of World War II, having previously posted on X that Nazis occupying Paris were 'infinitely preferable' to the LGBT-infused Last Supper parody at the Paris

Olympics in 2024. Both points are objectively and outrageously wrong.

In my view it's also woke to walk around thinking you can't trust any institution because everything is controlled by shadowy elites who have conspired against the people to protect their own interests. As with 'institutional racism' and 'systems of oppression', it's a way of denying your own personal responsibility and also your ability to make things better. Plenty of life's big winners have been down on their luck and have to overcome adversity on the road to greatness. None of them started out saying 'the system is rigged so there's no point trying'.

Social media has been an essential companion for woke and we have to find better ways of handling it. The reason why woke tactics are lingering in a post-woke world is because we're still taking our cues from this digital zoo. There are more than a billion posts every single day, meaning bizarro claims like 'Churchill was worse than Hitler' inevitably stand out among the cat videos. Local arguments can become global causes within hours and there is instant access to a mass morality mob that condemns brands, celebs and right-wing uncles before they even realise who they've offended.

Before social media it would have taken years for mad ideas like 'privilege' and 'my truth' to spread around the world and they would probably have been stopped in their tracks by normal people asking them what the hell they are talking about. Now they spread like wildfire, as does completely false information designed to stoke rage.

It's also tribal by design. The whole machine is built to retain your eyeballs for as long as possible and both conflict and confirmation of your righteousness are addictive. You get so used to seeing your own views shouted back at you that a dissenting opinion is treated like an enemy soldier sneaking into your camp. At the same time you're bombarded by idyllic images of people pretending they've achieved maximum prosperity, which only compounds the fury.

There are few things more pathetic and irritating than seeing a rash post by a lunch break political commentator turn into a pitchfork mob attack. If I was world king I would instantly ban anybody who researches where an 'offensive' tweeter works and tags their employer, asking 'is *this* what your brand stands for?' Does it really bring you joy if a man or woman loses their job because they said something mean on Facebook?

If the answer is yes, you are much more of a problem for society than the mean tweets guy who probably just needs to put down his phone on the taxi ride back from the pub. There's a reason why the kid in school who raised their hand to say 'miss ... miss, look ... Piers is chewing gum' was severely numerically challenged in the popularity department. Plenty of true malice and hatred and bigotry exists online, as it does in the real world. But we used to be able to tell the difference between idiots and ideologues.

None of this represents how we interact with objectionable people in real life. And the way we behave online is a lousy guide to the genuine opinions we have on the things that really matter to us. After a few minutes of real human chatter over a cup of coffee, or preferably a foaming pint of beer, you are very likely to discover that you actually agree on quite a few things – or that you don't really care after all.

Timeline obsession has also encouraged the lazy idea that fighting for what you believe in now means strapping in for a big outrage session on the smartphone. You didn't physically do anything to help anybody today, but you marched into battle on X with a Ukrainian flag and pronouns in bio. You 'owned the libs' or solved racism with your black square on Instagram. Congratulations, now for goodness sake go for a walk or call your mother.

Barack Obama hit the nail on the head all the way back in 2019. 'I get a sense among certain young people on social media that the way of making change is to be as judgemental as possible about other people,' he said. 'If I tweet or hashtag about how you didn't do something right or used the wrong verb, then I can sit back and feel pretty good about myself because "Man did you see how woke I was? I called you out!"' He also summed up the whole folly of cancel culture with a very simple sentence that's worth remembering: 'People who do really good stuff have flaws.'

In our brave new world of common sense, we have to do a lot better and it starts with a reality check. Millions upon millions of posts are now by bots, sent out to harvest our wrath for clicks, which makes the whole thing feel like a total farce. AI has been quietly absorbing our insanity and learning to replicate it with disturbing accuracy. If we're not careful we'll find ourselves trapped as props in a world of warring AI chatbots, screaming at each other over AI-generated videos of AI characters. Not exactly a good use of our time and energy.

It's already capable of generating ever more lifelike content, which can very easily be used to create false realities. This is why I worry so much about any movement that is so convinced of its moral superiority that all means are justified in recruiting supporters and silencing critics. It already feels like people are watching two different movies with the same characters and the same sets but wildly different storylines; directed by who they follow and who they watch. The next moralistic movement will have some scary new weapons in its armoury and needs to be met by a wall of very human gut instincts.

The best defence is to trust your boring inner moderate who can see a bit of good in most things and doesn't want to ostracise and destroy the other side. The great thing about common sense is that most of us are born with it. Sometimes it's overwhelmed by emotion or persuasion, but there is still a little voice in our heads that says, 'hang on a second, this is bullshit'. Most people don't need to be taught that women do not have penises or that male boxers shouldn't be fighting women, we just know because the little voice tells us. Listen to it.

A bit of perspective helps too. In a thousand years, humans might be living under the rule of an AI. world president that distributes all of our resources for us and makes every decision instantaneously by algorithm. We might be dispersed across multiple planets, as Elon Musk believes, having colonised faraway rocks to guarantee the survival of our species. But if there is anything like history as we know it today, pieced together with fragments of the lives we leave behind, every bloodcurdling argument and culture war will still be long forgotten.

Ancient Egyptians are mostly acclaimed for their ingenious and improbable engineering of the Pyramids, their gilded tombs and their hieroglyphics. The Vikings are defined by their masterful seafaring, their pioneering trade and their brutal conquests. There is no doubt they all debated furiously about who was in charge and how they should organise themselves, but it's not the stamp they left on the world, nor how they are defined.

History will have a similarly slimmed-down view about all of us. For all the billions of dollars spent every four years on changing the US president and for all of the emotional angst expended on social media wars about gender-neutral toilets, none of it is making a dent.

This is the era where men and women of genius made computer chips smaller than ants that ended up being smarter than us, and robots that can build space-travelling satellites without ever making a mistake or needing a cup of tea. The invention of the internet is not about photos of avocado toast or your hot take on Justin Bieber's meltdown but the miracle of instant access to all of the world's information. Your avocados won't even be remembered by dinnertime.

So, with our total and utter irrelevance cheerily established we can freely concentrate on making the best of our short time on earth, which matters deeply to us even if not our future AI overlords. Change has to start with our young people because they are going to be here for a lot longer than us – and lately we've been setting them a truly dreadful example.

Children have been repeatedly and shamefully used as cannon fodder in the culture war – almost invariably for the gratification of adults. Some of the examples of this seem quaint or ridiculous, such as the fad of 'gender-creative parenting' in which idiotic adults indulge themselves by creating a faux reality, devoid of all gender norms, to see what the child comes up with on their own. But it gets a lot less quaint and a lot more reprehensible when you look at what the pandering caused.

The national NHS review of gender services by Dr Hilary Cass was a bombshell development in the trans debate that has rippled across the entire world. There was nothing nuanced about its findings. Major medical bodies were rushing confused children into taking powerful puberty-blocking hormones on the basis that reinforcing their gender curiosity was the best thing for their mental health. But the review made clear there is simply no strong evidence to support that and plenty to suggest that it causes life-changing problems.

Hundreds of children who said they were transgender were rushed onto hormones at the UK's Tavistock gender clinic, despite having very complex mental health problems including trauma and autism. Many of them were simply gay. They were sped down this pathway of drastic and permanent physical changes because of aggressive lobbying by lunatics who weaponised the empathy or cowardice of everybody else. The clinic has now been shut down and the UK, along with a raft of liberal countries like Sweden, Denmark and France, have banned puberty blockers, apart from in exceptional circumstances, for anybody below the age of 18.

It's horrifying that some people justified literal medical experimentation on kids on the basis of pseudo-scientific kindness and in fear of being labelled 'transphobic'. A very small number of children do suffer genuine gender dysphoria and really do feel they were born in the wrong body. Many of them are simply confused and need time to figure it all out, which applies to almost everything they experience as adolescents.

One person who has now 'de-transitioned' back to their birth sex wrote: 'Had the recommendations from the Cass Review been implemented when I transitioned, in particular the recommendation of waiting until the age of 25, I never would have transitioned. I grew out of gender dysphoria by the age of 22, but had my genitals amputated by then.'

The medicalising of kids is the most visceral and damaging example of prioritising self-identity and 'lived experience' over cold facts. It ticked all of the usual boxes for woke campaigners. These children were portrayed as a vulnerable, marginalised group whose identity was being stifled by the dated 'power structures' controlled by patriarchal straight men. Plenty of people were suckered into joining the crusade because it masqueraded as compassionate, but it's now beyond doubt that it was anything but kind. In society as in life, no matter the arguments we're having among ourselves we should keep children well away from it.

The woke mindset of pitting marginalised groups against their apparent tormentors is deeply divisive, but it appeals to some primal urges. For most of human history we roved around in tight-knit tribes who believed, with some justification, that spearing the people who looked different was key to survival. But those tribes also depended on one fundamentally human and positive thing that we've gradually abandoned – community. Humans are built for helping each other out to survive and to stay happy. But most of our rewards and satisfaction now come from a very specific brand of selfishness.

Today's young people may be the first in human history to be taught that self-identity is more important than their role in a group. Your loyalty is no longer to your family and neighbours but to those who identify as you do. Your sense of meaning is no longer inherited but discovered on your 'personal journey'. Go find yourself, be who you want to be, live your truth, cut out the toxic people – even if they're family. Choose from the vibrant panoply of endless genders and hunker down on the internet with people who agree with everything you say, on a platform that is literally based on pictures of your own face and telling people all about you.

'Content creator' is the fastest-growing type of profession in the US. Kids used to dream of being astronauts, albeit not the Katy Perry kind. Now two-thirds of Gen Z want to be an online influencer. There is no 'job' more narcissistic than one that consists entirely of talking about yourself all day and assuming there is a vast appetite for discovering what jeans you're going to wear and what you're eating for breakfast. Feminists fought hard against women having to stay at home and look pretty, only for many of their kids to dream of emulating Kim Kardashian so they can stay at home and look pretty.

In the palm of every child's hand is a video games arcade, a casino, a shopping mall, a raging culture war, a cinema, a 24-hour radio station playing only their favourite music, a gallery filled with photographs of everybody else's massive success and a lifetime's supply of pornography. No wonder they're hooked on screens, increasingly anxious and addicted to instant gratification.

Consequently many young people now expect everything good in life to be available immediately and handed to them on a plate. Preferably a fancy square one, decorated with pink salt and chilli flakes for Instagram. A couple of years ago aspiring student medics at New York University signed a petition against their tutor, an esteemed professor called Maitland Jones. His apparent offence was making the organic chemistry class too difficult so that too many of them were failing. Instead of telling them to get off TikTok and read a book, the university responded by firing the professor.

I don't entirely blame young people for this attitude. They are the first kids to have been raised on woke culture and smartphones, and there is also clearly a failure of parenting and role models at play. The students who were so shocked to discover that organic chemistry is actually quite difficult are the product of a society in which parents called their infant children 'heroes' and handed out participation trophies for finishing in last place. If you slap trigger warnings on *Dumbo* and *The Jungle Book*, don't be surprised when the kids grow up to be horrified – as millions have been – by old episodes of *Friends* on Netflix.

Jennifer Aniston responded to a huge viral trend of Gen Z teenagers decrying the classic sitcom as 'sexist, transphobic and lacking diversity' by lamenting the sanitised mollycoddling mess we created to protect them. '[In the past] you could joke about a bigot and have a laugh,' she said. 'That was hysterical, and it was educating people on how ridiculous people were. Now we're not allowed to do that ... everyone is far too divided.'

We used to talk about fussy 'helicopter parents' who hovered around their children and took an unhealthy interest in solving all of their problems for them. Now those parents are driving tanks, rolling over anybody who stands in the way of their child's progress and firing missiles at their enemies. CNBC reported that a quarter of Gen Z jobseekers have turned up at a job interview with a parent in tow. Employers told another survey that 15 per cent of them had received complaints about not giving an applicant the job – from their mother or father.

Everybody wants the very best for their children but that includes allowing them to experience rejection, failure and disappointment. The real world is full of it. The more you learn to overcome it, the more successful you will be. I've read hundreds of stories about how Gen Z workers are prone to laziness, taking offence and showing an obvious lack of interest in their jobs. But maybe it's because we raised them to believe they should follow their wildest dreams and that everything falls apart if they don't get into an elite university. Of course they're going to be uninspired by a middling office job that gives them no prospect of owning a house until they're 40.

Telling young people the truth is a good place to start, even when it hurts. I don't mind getting the ball rolling. Less than 1 per cent of all the aspiring 'influencers' will ever wield enough influence to actually make a decent living, ranking it alongside modelling, elite sports and acting. I'm a firm believer in massive ambition and dreaming big, but the gratification and glory in life doesn't often come with Instagram glamour. The smartest strategy is to find something you're actually very good at and do a lot more of that.

As Professor Scott Galloway said: 'Anyone who tells you to follow your passion is already rich. You know what you're going to become passionate about? Making a shit ton of money so you can take care of your kids and your parents.' In other words, your community. The ones you forgot on the meandering self-gratifying quest to find your identity.

There is no shame in mastering traditional skills – quite the opposite. For all the talk of AI replacing vast numbers of human jobs, it's going to be a very long time before a chatbot can lay down a carpet or fix a burst water main. And clearly you'd be far happier and far richer as the world's greatest plumber than the world's lousiest TikToker.

Colleges and universities are not the holy grail, more so now than ever. I'd always encourage all young people to get the best education they can, but we should also be honest about the crisis in our universities so we can focus on fixing it. Many have become seething hotbeds of vicious woke intolerance. Their interest in preparing young people for the real world has declined at the same pace as their fees have rocketed. Students and their fee-paying parents are now viewed as 'customers' and the customer is always right – quite literally.

The number of UK graduates getting first-class honours more than doubled in a decade. About 45 per cent of students get an 'A' at US colleges compared to 15 per cent 50 years ago. This doesn't seem to have been caused by an explosion of intelligence, discipline and wisdom.

Universities are supposed to be the engine rooms of intellect; a place for genius to flourish and for debate to stretch the boundaries of human understanding. Instead they've become 'safe spaces' *from* ideas instead of *for* them. Conservative or 'transphobic' feminists routinely have their speaking gigs cancelled amid howls of protest or are met with abusive placard-waving mobs who attempt to drown out their heretic opinions. Woke was born in our universities and they will be the place where the last rites take the longest to be read.

Courses and reading lists have been sanitised or labelled with 'trigger warnings' on the assumption that students are hopelessly infantile and vulnerable. Aberdeen warns that Shakespeare's *A Midsummer Night's Dream* contains 'classism' while Greenwich censures Orwell's *Nineteen Eighty-Four* over its scenes of 'self-injurious behaviour and animal cruelty'. Budding crime scene investigators at

Exeter University are warned that their forensic science course includes 'material of a graphic nature'. Surely that's what they're paying for?

Hundreds of US professors have been sanctioned or fired for expressing opinions that challenge the cosy campus consensus or risk upsetting the students; a disturbing and worsening trend that has been tracked in detail by the First Amendment watchdog FIRE.

Academics have always tended to be moderate lefty idealists, but there's been a mass deportation of conservative opinions. Political scientist Samuel Abrams calculated that the ratio of liberal to conservative professors has ballooned by 350 per cent since 1984, meaning there are nine raving Marxists for every curmudgeonly conservative. According to the *College Fix*, 96 per cent of political donations from Ivy League faculties go to Democrats, compared with 4 per cent to Republicans. So much for diversity! It's a perfect storm of increasingly woke-infused students meeting a wall of woke professors in an institution that bends to their every woke whim to keep the cash flowing.

Having said that, a revelatory recent study by the psychologists Forest Romm and Kevin Waldman showed that a huge proportion of American students are actually faking their own wokeness. A survey of over 1,400 students at two of the top two universities in the US – Northerwestern and Michigan – revealed that nearly 88 per cent of students were exaggerating their progressive views to further their social or professional prospects. In fact, four out of five said that they had actually submitted coursework that misrepresented their personal views simply to grease the wheels of their professors.

There is nothing new or surprising about students being liberal and idealistic either. The worrying new development is the failure to prepare them for the impending reality in which many of their ideas will be robustly challenged by people who vehemently disagree with them. You can't possibly know that you're right about anything if you systematically plug your ears and squawk over every different point of view. But universities have become giant echo chambers that only allow one uncompromising woke worldview.

The fundamentalist intolerance on elite campuses was laid bare in the aftermath of the 7 October 2023 massacre in Israel. Protests erupted long before Israel's bombardment and blockade in Gaza became morally indefensible. The Hamas terrorists were literally still in the middle of carrying out their barbaric rampage when Yale's professor Zareena Grewal posted that 'Israel is a murderous, genocidal settler state and Palestinians have every right to resist through armed struggle.' On 8 October, more than 30 student groups at Harvard signed a statement holding the Israeli regime 'entirely responsible for all unfolding violence'.

Dozens of US campuses were overwhelmed by occupations and disorder, which quickly spawned replica protests in the UK and Australia. Many Jewish students and staff were threatened or abused. Some were physically attacked. Viral clips showed demonstrators proudly chanting 'burn Tel Aviv to the ground' and 'Hamas we love you, we support your rockets too'. Calls for 'intifada revolution' became the motto of the student protest movement; an explicit reference to violent and deadly Palestinian uprisings.

Three top university presidents were hauled before Congress to explain their total failure to plug the spigot of overt antisemitism. Harvard's Claudine Gay was asked directly whether 'calling for the genocide of Jews' violated the university's rules on harassment and bullying. Inexplicably and shamefully, she answered that 'it can be depending on the context'.

Try replacing the word 'Jews' with 'black people' or 'Muslims' and see how much context is needed. Claudine Gay was ultimately forced to resign as president over claims she had plagiarised and stolen ideas in her research. A copy of this book is in the mail in the hope she copies one or two of mine.

This repellant and dogmatic racism could only have flourished unchecked in this fairytale world of 'oppressors' and the 'oppressed', which universities have baked into their teaching for years. Here were some of the most privileged people on planet earth, raging against the only multi-ethnic democracy in the Middle East and in support of a regime that violently crushes protests and imprisons homosexuals. It only makes sense in the self-loathing story of marginalised heroes and privileged villains.

To be clear, there is nothing wrong with protesting against war. I've reminded many of the pro-Palestine guests on my show that I led the national campaign against invading Iraq as editor of the *Daily Mirror*. The problem is that we've given young people such a basic and uncompromising framework for understanding the world that many felt justified in racially abusing Jewish people and supporting literal terrorists.

The new Trump administration quickly revoked the visas of hundreds of foreign students it said were proven to have openly supported Hamas, which triggered a fist-waving backlash about free speech. But if you seriously think it's a free speech issue, ask yourself whether there would be any complaints about, say, a white British student being deported for harassing black people and supporting the KKK. Of course there wouldn't. America's First Amendment is the most powerful legal protector of free speech anywhere in the world – but it doesn't cover incitement to violence and there is no constitutional right to a student visa.

Universities can be quite simple. They should be centres of excellence that give young people the facilities to carry out groundbreaking research and the skills to create economic value. That's it. Instead they've appointed themselves as agents of change and social engineers whose main goal is to eliminate injustice and promote diversity.

They're also overflowing with do-gooders who are not doing anything good. In the US and UK, most universities employ as many 'administrators' overseeing things like diversity quotas, compliance and marketing as they do teaching staff. Yale and Harvard ludicrously now have more administrators than students.

Administrators at Cardiff University banned phrases like 'piece of cake' for being 'too British' and at Leeds

University they barred the words 'mum and dad' because they are so wickedly gendered.

I don't claim to be an expert on education reform and I don't particularly want to be. But it seems like a good place to start would be sacking literally all of these people. Classes on white supremacy should be replaced by classes on the importance of free speech. Every student should have to specify the social cause they are most passionate about and write an essay from the perspective of someone who thinks they are totally wrong. And anybody who 'de-platforms' a guest speaker by hurling abuse at them should be promptly de-platformed from the university.

If only there was a University of Common Sense, or a course named 'Introduction to Contemporary Piers Morgan Theory'. Perhaps there should be. Many future business and political leaders study Philosophy, Politics and Economics (PPE). I'm calling the following programme PP-Me and it's open to adults and youngsters of all abilities who want to get ahead and for the world to be a bit less nuts. These are my 13 lessons for making your own luck and ensuring woke is buried for good.

Chapter 15

THE 13 LIFE LESSONS FOR MAKING YOUR OWN LUCK

Instead of the bombardment of simpering confessionals, I want to see a constant barrage of high-profile people talking about strength and solutions.

1. PESSIMISTS ARE UNLUCKY

'I find that the harder I work, the more luck I seem to have.'

America's third president and Founding Father Thomas Jefferson is often credited with this incisive observation, but sadly there's no evidence he actually said it. With that in mind, I'll go with it. After deciding to write this book I wrote down a list of life lessons in my diary as an antidote to the bad habits we've collectively been learning. I've knowingly whittled it down to a 'lucky' 13 – partly to make a petty point about our pointless pessimism, but also because they have generally been very lucky for me.

Luck is just a way of describing the successes and failures that appear to be created by random chance. By definition, you can't control luck itself. But you can absolutely control your skills, knowledge, preparedness and attitude, all of which are essential for spotting good luck when it happens and rebounding from bad luck with equal vigour. Having a fire in your belly and high expectations for yourself is like buying twenty lottery tickets instead of one. Chance does all the rest.

The illusionist Derren Brown made a TV show called *The Secret of Luck*. It featured a crude experiment in which a £50 note was placed in plain sight on the street to see who would pick it up. Most of the people who walked past, either suspiciously or obliviously, were later assessed to be pessimistic people who dwelled on their misfortune. Optimistic, open-minded people walked off with fatter wallets.

If you're prone to going about life in a state of despondency – always expecting bad luck and feeling it's you against the world – you're proven to be less likely to spot opportunities and less prepared to take advantage of them. Ambitious, focused optimists will seize on the smallest crumb of an opportunity and fancy their chances at making it work. A confident optimist will think getting a shot at a job they're unqualified for is tremendous good luck. A pessimist will just fret about embarrassing themselves or find reasons they're unable to do it.

Studies show that people who think of themselves as unlucky are far more likely to believe in the proverbial bad luck superstitions like breaking mirrors, walking under ladders and Friday the 13th. Neither doom-laden pessimists nor giddy optimists are seeing cold hard reality, but they're choosing to interpret the world in different ways, which can directly change whether they feel lucky or not.

Take Friday the 13th, the mythical day of doom that many English-speaking cultures believe is a harbinger of inevitable woe. The belief is so widespread that there's a word for people who are genuinely petrified of it – paraskevidekatriaphobia. I'd just be petrified of having to say it on TV. There's no specific reason or heinous event that inspires this fallacy. It has been cobbled together with circumstantial evidence over a period of centuries.

Most people now yearn for Fridays like hungry dogs at an empty bowl, but Christians are traditionally less enthusiastic. Jesus was crucified on a Friday, which is why Catholics see it as a day of confessional penance. Medieval stories proclaimed Friday to be the day that Adam and Eve wolfed the forbidden fruit. The Knights Templar were arrested and tortured en masse on Friday the 13th in October 1307.

Loathing for the number 13 has more practical origins. The number 12 is neatly divisible by six different numbers, making it a useful measure of completeness. We have 12 months in a year, 12 hours on a clock, 12 lunar cycles, 12 zodiac signs, 12 days of Christmas, 12 inches in a foot, 12 eggs in a box. There were 12 Olympian gods, 12 Apostles of Jesus and 12 Tribes of Israel. We even put 12 people on a jury. The European Union's blue flag has 12 gold stars to symbolise completeness and unity.

What has the number 13 ever done for anyone? It's stubbornly divisible only by one and itself, making it a fairly useless measurement, and it seems to come along and rudely spoil the order of everything. Judas was the 13th guest at the Last Supper. Arsenal won the league title for the 13th time in 2004 and, sure enough, it has never happened again. I rest my case. Fear of Friday the 13th comes from the unholy matrimony of a day and a number that people don't like very much. But obviously it's all a load of cobblers.

In Spain, Greece and Latin America it's Tuesday the 13th that gets people's knickers in a twist. Italians don't like Friday the 17th. In China, South Korea and Japan the word for number four sounds like 'death' which means April the 4th is considered a good day to avoid heavy machinery. People in Thailand are scared of getting a haircut on Wednesdays, forcing most barbershops to close. If all of this sounds daft, which it is, consider that it's basically the same premise as blaming 'bad luck' for all of your own misfortunes.

If you're a glass-half-full type of person, as I am, then Friday the 13th is a magnificent day for humanity. President Lyndon B. Johnson signed an historic executive order banning employment discrimination by sex on Friday the 13th – a huge stride forward in the battle for gender equality. Evelyn Kilgore was certified as the first female flight instructor on Friday 13 October 1939.

Freedom-fighting union forces began toppling the Confederate stronghold at Fort Fisher on Friday 13 January 1865. US forces defeated the Japanese in a bruising and deadly melee dubbed the Battle of Friday the 13th in 1942, a crucial strategic turning point in World War II. The glorious Mediterranean island of Malta declared independence from the Brits on Friday 13 December 1974.

American adventurer Roy Chapman Andrews discovered dinosaur eggs while digging near Mongolia's Flaming Cliffs on Friday 13 July 1923. It was the first concrete evidence that dinosaurs laid eggs and is still considered one of the biggest breakthroughs in paleontology. Andrews was made director of the American Museum of Natural History.

NASA announced on Friday 13 November 2009 that a probe had discovered at least 25 gallons of water on the moon, sparking excitable talk of lunar space ports or colonies. Future missions could now be powered by oxygen, drinking water and even rocket fuel made from lunar liquid.

Harry Chandler, the publisher of the *LA Times*, chose Friday 13 July in 1923 to unveil his giant 'Hollywoodland' sign on Mount Lee in Los Angeles. Originally planned as a temporary advertisement for his real estate development, its abbreviated form is now one of the most iconic landmarks in the world.

Beloved British rocker Ozzy Osbourne (RIP) and his band Black Sabbath released their self-titled debut album on Friday 13 February 1970. Critics savaged it, but it's now regarded as an all-time classic that singularly invented the genre of heavy metal. 'You think back to that time, it was all about love, peace and bullshit,' Ozzy said later. 'I was coming out with some demonic overtones, which was a new angle, I suppose.'

Taylor Swift chose Friday the 13th to release her Eras Tour movie and says 13 is her lucky number. Given that the movie raked in more than $260 million at the box office, she might have a point. Nintendo released the first Super Mario Bros video game on Friday 13 September 1985. The portly Italian plumber has made over $60 billion for the company since then, becoming one of the most successful media franchises in history.

There is even some evidence to suggest that Friday the 13th may actually be one of the safest dates in the calendar because so many superstitious people choose not to fly or take extra care on the roads. In 2008, the Dutch Centre for Insurance Statistics reported that insurers habitually receive fewer accident reports when Friday falls on the 13th than any typical Friday. The final and most obvious point about Friday the 13th is that it's always the day before Saturday, which is usually a very good thing.

I could obviously compile a long list of disasters and tragedies on Friday the 13th. Plenty of other people already have. The point is that you can spot negative and positive patterns in everything if you look for them, including your own life, all based on the same basic reality. But the patterns are about your attitude, not luck.

Luck is the stuff that just happens. Actor Seth MacFarlane was supposed to be on American Airlines Flight 11, which crashed into the North Tower on 9/11, but missed it after a night of heavy drinking. Maureen Wilcox bought tickets for each of the Rhode Island and Massachusetts lotteries and chose the exact winning numbers for both. Unfortunately her Rhode Island numbers won in Massachusetts and her Massachusetts numbers won in Rhode Island, so she won diddly-squat.

Nobody can do anything about pure luck. But we can do a hell of a lot to increase our chances of success and our optimism about spotting and using good luck when it happens. The last few years have been all about pessimism, wallowing and pinpointing the reasons why things are irredeemably bleak or finding the societal barriers standing in the way of achievement. It's a vicious circle of doom. The antidote? Choose your superstitions wisely. If you're going to believe in something without evidence, why not believe in your own capability to create a bit of good fortune through preparation, optimism and action?

A few years ago I spent the day with the late General Colin Powell at the National War College in Washington DC. Powell was an inspirational leader who fought his way up from the humblest origins to become one of the most powerful men on the planet. He showed me his own set of rules for life and I've always remembered them as I essentially agreed with every one. Number 13, ironically, was: 'Perpetual optimism is a force multiplier.'

2. TELL US WHAT YOU REALLY THINK

Despite the endless concerted efforts to banish me from the media and polite society, speaking up for what I believe in and sharing my honestly held opinions has generally always put me right where I want to be in life. And that just so happens to be exactly where I am.

Unless you really are a raving Nazi or a hateful bigot, nothing good can come of censoring yourself in the name of appeasing others. The whole world is a seething mass of people who want to control the direction of society, politics and culture. Taking part in that debate is the spice of life and the bedrock of democracy. But it shouldn't always be a team sport.

Modern tribalism often boils down to the idea that people who want everything to be more liberal or more conservative should unite on all things, even when they disagree, because defeating the other side is the sole mission. It's insincere, ruinous for debate and it's the main reason why politics has become so hopelessly hate-filled and partisan. Neither 'side' can be entirely right, or wrong, about absolutely everything.

The woke movement was so intransigently certain of its righteousness that any dissenting view had to be shamed and silenced. And it was strictly a set menu, not an all-you-can-eat buffet. 'Allies' had to be all in on the whole package with no exceptions allowed. That's why otherwise sensible liberal politicians found themselves defending puberty blockers for children and there were marches under the banner of 'Queers for Palestine'.

Many people got uncomfortably comfortable with the idea that a person's career or social standing could be wrecked as easily as they are blocked or muted on social media. It will take a long time for everybody to shed the symptoms of Long Woke, but the recovery starts with staying true to your personal beliefs and not blindly following the pack.

The Israel–Hamas war is a perfect case in point. For a long time I was berated for spouting 'Israeli talking points' and ridiculously accused of being an Islamophobe over my coverage. That was because in the aftermath of 7 October I felt very strongly that Israel had a right and a duty to respond with force to a heinous terrorist attack. I interviewed and hosted more pro-Palestine guests than any prominent show in the world, but I expected them to condemn the atrocities as a basic test of their humanity and their ability to have a reasoned discussion.

My patience with Israel's government wore increasingly thin over a long period, but the collapse of the ceasefire in March 2025, followed by a punishing blockade that pushed thousands beyond the brink of famine, was the final straw. The war in Gaza now looked aimless, punitive and callous.

I turned up the heat on Israeli officials appearing on my show, most notably in an interview with the UK ambassador in which I asked her 17 times how she could state with supreme confidence how many terrorists Israel had killed but have absolutely no idea how many children had died in the onslaught. She had 17 ways of ignoring the question.

The response was a barrage of people accusing me of spouting 'Hamas talking points' and ridiculously accusing me of being an antisemite. Many of the same people who cheered my combative interviews with pro-Palestine guests now said their very presence on my show was evidence of some deep-seated loathing of Jewish people. There were hilarious demands for me to be fired from my show, which I own.

What this told me, as a journalist and a human being, is that I was getting it right. My opinions change when the facts change, as they should do. I'm not interested in picking a 'side' and passing its purity tests. I'm committed to following my instincts and keeping a firm grip on my own sense of right and wrong. It's far more disturbing and unusual to have the same intractable worldview for years on end and never consider that you might be wrong.

Two things happen when I share a big opinion on anything. The first is that thousands of people who disagree with it tell me that nobody cares about my opinion, even though they invariably follow my opinions on social media or watch my opinion-led show. The second wave is from smart and sensible people who disagree with me but want to explain why. Sometimes their competing evidence makes me doubly sure of myself. Sometimes they make a lot of sense and I'll hone my views accordingly. That's exactly how debate should work. Tribal opinions are like big ugly boulders. My views are evolving, and continue to be chiselled and sculptured masterfully from the rock.

As editor of the *Daily Mirror* I led the campaign against the invasion of Iraq, putting us on a collision course with the Labour government we'd backed. I was regularly summoned to Downing Street for hours of fractious and often bad-tempered meetings with Tony Blair and spin doctor Alastair Campbell, but our campaign continued long after the war began. Some readers deserted us for papers adopting the blinkered patriotism expected by the government, but I stayed true to my own values. Neither

Tony Blair nor I came out of that period smelling of roses, but only one of us is blamed for the biggest foreign policy disaster in modern British history.

The Casey Review into the UK grooming scandal, which finally forced the government to order a national inquiry, has an entire chapter on 'denial'. Dame Louise Casey found that powerful officials had the data to prove suspects were mostly Asian men but ordered it to be covered up as they feared stoking racial tensions or being accused of racism themselves.

Their cowardice and negligence led to incalculable suffering that carried on for years after it could have been stopped. But they were enabled by people much further down the food chain who blotted out the word 'Pakistani' with Tipp-Ex in paperwork and chose to say nothing.

'If good people don't grasp difficult things, bad people will, and that's why we have to do it as a society,' Dame Louise said. The cover-up only fuelled and emboldened racists and hate-mongers by allowing them to dominate the narrative and obliterating public trust. I shudder to think about the misery and angst that could have been prevented by more people having the courage to simply say what they could see.

Fortunately, most of us will never find ourselves in anything like that position, but we can still apply the same lessons to making the world a more honest and interesting place. Be polite and respectful but severely allergic to bullshit. Follow your gut instinct instead of the herd and never be afraid to say what you mean. We're all grown-ups, we can take it. I'd rather be jabbed in the stomach than stabbed in the back and I suspect most people feel the same way.

3. KEEP POUNDING

> *'The world ain't all sunshine and rainbows. It's a very mean and nasty place and I don't care how tough you are, it will beat you to your knees and keep you there permanently if you let it ... But it ain't about how hard you hit. It's about how hard you can get hit and keep moving forward ... That's how winning is done.'*

Sorry, Sir Winston, but Rocky Balboa's rousing monologue to his sulking brattish son may be my favourite motivational speech in modern history. The stirring speech in the middle of the sixth *Rocky* movie was written by Sylvester Stallone himself and delivered with a savagely authentic intensity. I saw it for the first time almost 20 years ago and have been quoting it, word-for-word, to my own kids for just as long.

First, it's a reality check. Life will inevitably hurt you and disappoint you, but that doesn't make you special because it applies equally to a crown prince and a milkman. We're all going to take a beating at some point, but failure itself is not fatal. The world is universally unfair and unpredictable, but we are not hapless passengers on a dead-end journey. It will bring you to your knees – if you let it.

Second, it flips the script on what it takes to win. Success is really about overcoming failure, not avoiding it. Dominance is impossible without perseverance. Every champion has to go through hell to reach the top and the world is full of extremely talented failures who couldn't stand the heat.

The difference between being good and great, or between being great or the greatest, is measured in the ability to bounce back from disappointment and the relentless pursuit of self-improvement. Resilience is the powerful combination of mastering failure and working tirelessly until you've done everything as well as you possibly can. It means diverting the energy from brooding into improving instead. And if that all sounds like hard work, it's supposed to.

Instead of celebrating resilience and graft, our culture has succumbed to the systemic indulgence of wallowing. Young people are bombarded with information and ideas about things that might be wrong with them and there is viral currency in victimhood. Speaking 'your truth' is brave and courageous. Celebrities are lauded for revealing their 'mental health journey'. It's 'OK to not be OK'. All of the social validation and rewards are for talking about pain and strife as if struggling itself is the end goal instead of the quest to overcome it.

Legendary actress Dame Joanna Lumley hit the nail on the head: 'This is a horrible thing to say but I think the mental health thing is being overplayed at the moment because anybody who's even remotely sad says they have got mental problems. You go, "This is what is called being human." When someone dies and you grieve, that's human. You're not mentally ill.'

I always keep in mind a short and simple poem by D. H. Lawrence about the uniquely human deficiency of self-pity. Somewhere along the way, in our world of ever-increasing prosperity and aspiration, we forgot the very natural instinct to just keep moving forwards:

I never saw a wild thing
sorry for itself.
A small bird will drop frozen dead from a bough
without ever having felt sorry for itself.

Instead of the bombardment of simpering confessionals, I want to see a constant barrage of high-profile people talking about strength and solutions. It's about saying yes, bad things happened to me too, but here's what I did about them and here's how I used them to come back stronger than I was before. That's the way to inspire people who are down on their luck.

I spend a lot of time listening to all of my children about problems they're facing and issues they need help with. I never diminish what they're going through, but I do always come back to the idea that, whatever it is, they have to push through it. You can either give up or keep pounding. Both options may end in failure, but only one of them gives you any hope of avoiding it.

I was raised and influenced by strong women, my mother and grandmother especially, who refused to surrender to self-pity in the face of adversity. My grandmother endured the horrors of World War II but then spent the subsequent 70 years leading a fun-filled life and never complaining about it. I've tried to live my own life with the same attitude. I also think that working in journalism for my entire adult life has left me with a very thick skin for dealing with the simple fact that truly horrible things happen every single day.

That doesn't mean I haven't had my fair share of failures and disappointments. Mine are often played out on television and in newspapers, with whole bus loads of hecklers and haters arriving to dance on my professional grave. I was fired by the *Daily Mirror* after 10 years, I lost my primetime CNN show, I was forced out of *Good Morning Britain* in the Markle debacle. At each junction it was only other people who thought the setbacks were catastrophic. I viewed them as opportunities, and every time I've managed to come back stronger.

I take a lot of inspiration from the sporting world because these are men and women who truly understand resilience. From the early morning training in the thick of winter to the formative years spent snubbing social opportunities and the anguish over injuries and defeat, every great champion has to learn to suffer and keep pushing through it.

Cristiano Ronaldo is still banging in goals at the age of 40 after a record-breaking career in which he's won almost every trophy and honour in football. He's the greatest player of all time in the world's most popular sport.

He's able to keep doing it because he has never lost any of his desire to win. Failure still gnaws at his soul. He has made enough money to live like a king for a dozen lifetimes without ever lifting a finger but still subjects himself to an extraordinary daily routine of physical conditioning that would make other professional athletes weep for mercy.

Ronaldo would be the first to arrive at the training ground and the very last to leave; dribbling the ball for thousands of kilometers on his own to perfect his trademark stepovers and pumping weights in the gym until the car park was emptied of its Maseratis. He studied YouTube clips of the skills he wanted to perfect and didn't stop practising until he had mastered them himself. And he is exactly the same today. As Cristiano Ronaldo himself puts it: 'If you think you're perfect already, then you never will be.'

In May 1954, the late Sir Roger Bannister became the first runner in history to run a mile in less than four minutes. As he thundered across the finishing line he collapsed from exhaustion and briefly lost his eyesight, overcome by the extreme exertion and euphoria of making history. Many years later I met him and asked if there was a single person or a quote that inspired him to keep pushing through hardship and disappointment until he finally did it. He told me this African proverb:

'Every morning in Africa a gazelle wakes up. It knows it must run faster than the fastest lion or it will not survive. Every morning a lion wakes up and it knows it must run faster than the slowest gazelle or it will starve. It doesn't matter whether

you are a lion or a gazelle. When the sun comes up, you better start running.'

I firmly believe that we're born resilient, as are the beasts of the natural world. All of the reasons we find to chip away at it are bad habits we learn from life. Wild animals are all just trying to survive and thrive, as we are. But a beaver doesn't get anxiety about having to build a dam. A magpie doesn't wish it was on a beach in Spain when it's carrying twigs to build a nest. I get rattled and disappointed, just like everybody else, but I know that when the sun comes up I'm going to start running.

4. JUST GET ON WITH IT

Procrastination is tempting because it delays responsibility. It's much more comfortable living in a world of fantastical possibilities. Telling people you're going to be the founder of a tech start-up or a top podcaster is much easier than actually trying to do it. You can appease your inner conquistador by setting all kinds of targets, which is really just another way of kicking the can further down the road.

Increasingly I find that even the smartest and most driven young people are oppressed by the tyranny of tomorrow. Everybody is making endless planning lists or talking about the big things they are going to do at some unspecified time in the future. In my experience this generally ends up being a big list of things you haven't done yet and another reason to feel gloomy. There's usually a parallel list of gloomy reasons why it's not going to work out.

We're surrounded by cunning methods of deferring action with time-wasting pacifiers. You're going to start jogging, but you're waiting for your new pair of Air Max trainers to be shipped from China. You're going to start your small business, but first you're reading a self-help book on capitalism. You haven't started writing your book yet, but you have told a lot of people how great it's going to be when you finish it.

The biggest barriers standing between you and having a go are the fear of failure and exertion aversion. Assuming you've thought carefully about what you want to do and have rational expectations (i.e. don't read this as my invitation to invest your life savings in a chocolate teapot factory), the worst that can happen is that you'll land on your face but learn something new and finish up more resilient than when you began.

The faster you start, the faster you'll find out if it's a winner or move on to the next thing. You can't start your dream job tomorrow morning, but you can start talking to people who already have it, belt out a sparkling new resume and get on the phone to some people who might know better than you do. You will feel a lot happier and a lot closer to achieving something than if you'd written all of those things on a to-do list to your frustrated future self.

I recently bumped into Prime Minister Sir Keir Starmer at a summer party and told him he should stop setting ludicrous targets. Starmer has made pledges the centrepiece of his PR strategy: 95 per cent green power by 2030,

92 per cent of patients waiting no longer than 18 weeks for planned treatment, 1.5 million new homes in England by the end of his term. It goes on and on.

Targets are the to-do lists of politics and government. They achieve only two things, neither of which are desirable. The first, like every list in the procrastinator's handbook, is to serve as a direct record of abject failure when they're inevitably not met. The second is to remind you how rotten everything is at the moment. Four months to have a dodgy tooth pulled out? Stop setting targets and get on with making things better.

Two weeks after my conversation with the Prime Minister his health secretary Wes Streeting popped up with an absurd target of making Britain 'fat free' – entirely cured of obesity – by 2035. Unless they're secretly plotting Trump-style mass deportations for all of Britain's porkers, there is more chance of me becoming Pope.

Plenty of people who know far more than I do about the psychology of massive success will tell you that it invariably takes a lot of time and patience. I don't disagree with that, but I would add this: the road to glory is winding, arduous and long, so you should be massively impatient about setting off as quickly as possible.

5. EMBRACE FOMO

When I was growing up I had no idea what my friends in the village were doing unless I was physically with them. My sons, on the other hand, were raised on a relentless stream of photographic evidence that all their friends and colleagues are having the time of their lives while they are not. This is what causes 'FOMO' – the fear of missing out – and it's the turbulent force behind the rising tide of anxiety and self-loathing.

FOMO is now spreading to older people as more people live their lives online. Thirty years ago you would have almost no way of finding out how estranged neighbours, schoolfriends or partners were getting on in life. Now you can access daily updates on how much money they're making, the exotic places they're travelling to and how their children are apparently destined for Mensa or the World Cup.

Social media is the envy machine at the heart of all this. Early adopters like the Kardashians set the tone by generating massive interest in carefully curated snapshots of their preposterously glamorous lives and wildly misleading representations of their own beauty. Now hundreds of millions of people plough much of their time and energy into presenting a selective reel of implausible perfection and maximum contentment.

I know this process very well because I'm not shy about posting selective evidence of my own indulgences in which I leave out the fact I woke up at 4 a.m. and have cramp in my leg. There's never a shortage of abusive wastrels who haven't left the house in a while lining up in the comments to express their X-rated scorn about my apparent satisfaction.

There's nothing wrong with comparing ourselves to other people and not much we can do about it either. Human beings learn many things by comparison. A child learns the difference between a purring kitten and a wild animal by comparing their eagerness to be patted on the head. The difference now is that social media has exponentially turbocharged the opportunities for comparison and completely distorted the expectations that go with it.

Jealousy is perfectly natural too. That's why dogs, chimps, ducks and dolphins all get jealous. It probably comes from the primal and existential urge to find a valuable mating partner and prevent anybody else from stealing them, as well as the basic need to have enough food to avoid death. The same goes for envy, which has been around for as long as humans have. Hunter-gatherers were prone to murdering tribesmen who received gifts, meaning they tended to share them out to avoid ending up on the wrong end of a long spear.

Used wisely, these natural urges can be a motivating force. If you know that you want what another person has, then you can start strategising about how you're going to get it for yourself. As a child at school I was a very good cricketer but a very ordinary athlete. So, I'd bask in the glory of once taking all ten wickets for just nine runs in a 1st XI match aged 12 but then face the comparative misery of the annual Sports Day where my running/jumping skills were extremely limited. I turned that festering fury into competitive energy. I was relentlessly determined to be the best of the losers and win the non-finallists race, which I did.

The big farce of FOMO is that so much of the accompanying bitterness and anxiety is caused by the envy of things that don't actually exist. Instagram is not reality. I'd compare it to an old travel brochure with photos of the piddling padding pool taken on an extremely wide lens and a massive building site cropped carefully out of the shot. Apply a common-sense filter. Remember that if they were having that much of a good time, they wouldn't be on their phones telling you about it.

Most importantly, remember that there's nothing you can do about anybody else. It's one of the oldest common-sense truths there is. You can only control what you're working on and how you are going to do it better. I might be envious of Channing Tatum's abs but he's not going to take me to the gym. My version of FOMO means 'Focus On Myself Only' and I'm extremely good at it.

6. THERE'S NO SUCH THING AS A LIFE HACK

You don't have to spend a long time online before running into a handsome young man sitting behind an obnoxiously large microphone with an idea or a product that will BLOW YOUR MIND or CHANGE YOUR LIFE. Shortcut syndrome is spreading like an infectious plague.

> 'It took me twenty years to learn this 5-minute routine that will save you 40 hours a week! Rich people never share this ONE trick! The five habits for solving 97.5 per cent of your problems! Rewire your brain for massive profit! How one inspiring sentence cured my depression! This simple everyday mistake is making you miserable, stupid, poor and fat!'

Most of the people selling you this babble have never succeeded at anything besides convincing people to click on their videos or download their apps. They're both a product and a symptom of a culture that increasingly demands instant gratification and, frankly, puts a lot of hard work into the avoidance of hard work.

There's no useful lesson in life that doesn't involve copious amounts of discipline, courage and perseverance. That's why it's a running theme in all of the lessons at the back of my notebook. The world is messy and unpredictable and nobody can draw you a straight line from rags to riches. There are only various different routes out of the thickets, all of which rely on repetition, focus and elbow grease.

Most people know that Thomas Edison perfected the lightbulb; a truly revolutionary innovation that brought enormous safety, comfort and efficiency to a gloomy world previously illuminated only by burning sticks of reeking whale fat and soot-spewing gas lamps. What most people don't know is that he often worked up to 22 hours a day and habitually slept in his laboratory. 'There is no substitute for hard work,' is how Edison put it.

On a single day in 1888 Edison wrote down 112 ideas for new inventions and he filed for patents at an average of once every eleven days in his adult life. Many of them were disastrous. The lightbulb and phonograph became global essentials, but his talking dolls were the stuff of nightmares, his concrete furniture was impractical and hideous, nobody ever used his electric pen, and it's unclear where he was going with his special ink for blind people.

'I have not failed,' Edison said. 'I've just found 10,000 ways that won't work.'

Author Malcolm Gladwell popularised the 10,000 hours rule. It's roughly the amount of time it takes to master a complex skill. A gifted pianist can tickle the keys with natural aplomb, but it takes thousands of hours of laborious repetition and painstaking practice to achieve mastery. Before The Beatles exploded as global megastars they spent more than a year in Hamburg playing gigs of up to eight hours long on all seven nights of the week. Ambition and talent are just the beginning. Toil and tedium come next.

There is only one shortcut made possible by 'life hacks'. They're a useful way of pinpointing what you want, which is no bad thing in a world of listless wallowing. It could be getting fit, getting rich, curbing your anxiety, improving your discipline, saving money, bolstering your social skills, speaking to attractive men or women, being a better leader, learner, father or mother. Knowing what you want to achieve is a head start. The next step is understanding that, whatever it is, you'll only get it through sacrifice.

Sporting champions know beyond any doubt that they want to win at all costs. The early morning training, the sobriety and the relentless physical pain are all made tolerable by that burning desire. Medical students slog through six years of study and then go to train, working poorly paid shifts of up to 28 hours, shunning all manner of social temptations, because they are hell-bent on making the grade. They know what they want and they want it so badly they will suffer to get it.

There's a reason why making sacrifices now to get something better in the future is the basis of most religions. It's an essential lesson in life. Ancient tribes no doubt wanted to gorge themselves on every sinew of every bison they poleaxed. But the ones who thrived came up with ingenious ways of drying or fermenting a few steaks so they could be sure of a meal if their hunting luck ran out.

Things get tough when there's no obvious or immediate reward. That's why I have every sympathy with the many young people who are putting their backs into everything they do but seem to get no closer to owning a house or even matching their parents' prosperity. That's where grit, faith and resilience come into it again, and the reason why the five-minute 'life hacks' are a lie. The faith part is believing it will get better even when all the evidence suggests otherwise, whether you're aiming for eternal paradise or a week in Cancun.

Clearly the key to unlocking it all is knowing what you want in the first place. If you're repeatedly attracted to 'life hacks' about growing your business, growing your confidence or growing your biceps then they've done you a bit of a favour. Now I'm afraid it's over to you and how much of today you're prepared to throw in the furnace to get what you want tomorrow.

7. BE A MAN!

Nothing signals virtue harder than a man turning on his own to prove what a refined and emotionally sophisticated comfort blanket he is. 'Women are better than men,' simpered Ryan Gosling, 'they're stronger, more evolved.' President Barack Obama fell squarely on his own metaphorical weapon at a female leadership conference, fawning: 'What I can say, pretty indisputably, is that you're better than us.' Actor Will Ferrell, a man, was the star booking at the Women in Entertainment Gala in 2023. He dutifully lamented 10,000 years of male failure and basked in the ovation as he asked: 'Isn't it just time for women to run the planet?'

Sorry to disappoint, but I won't be joining in with this ritual of self-humiliation. There's been more than enough manic man-bashing from woke gender-neutralisers and fuming feminists without men joining the pity party to burnish their own eligibility.

Men are the last remaining demographic for whom ridicule is not only accepted but encouraged, and we're now seeing real harm resulting from years of demanding men apologise for who they are.

Men and women are different. Until very recently that was accepted as an inalienable, common-sense fact. We know it because we can see it with our own eyes. Between my own children and my nieces and nephews, I've watched four boys and nine girls grow up. They're all unique and have vivid personalities, as we all do, but the boys and girls are naturally distinct. There are logical and evidence-based explanations for why.

Males have more testosterone, which makes them more likely to be zealously competitive and dominant in a group. They're usually stronger and have greater muscle mass for endurance and power. They're wired for taking bigger risks and drawn to fiercely defending their social status and their loved ones under threat from others. Most fundamental is the urge to become a provider or a breadwinner.

There's now a fast-rising number of couples or families in which the woman is making the most money. The man's instinct and role is still to step up and do the heavy lifting – often literally – so his partner can get on with succeeding herself. The point is feeling responsible for the household or family so all of the people in it can thrive on their own terms. Who could possibly have a problem with that?

Male aggression and strength have their downsides, obviously. Just because masculinity is inherently good it doesn't mean that all men are good too. There is clearly a societal problem with male violence, leading to women feeling unsafe on the streets. In the UK this has been fuelled by a series of shocking cases of violent male sexual attacks by police officers, whose subversion of their role as a protector makes their crimes even more abominable.

Across the world, men are far more likely to commit violent or sexual crimes. That's just a fact. But the overwhelming majority of men are not criminals. They're repulsed and angered by these crimes.

In a culture of condemning creeps and unwanted advances, I'm also prepared to die on the very lonely hill of defending male seduction. There's nothing sleazy about fancying women or wanting them to know about it. In fact it's somewhat fundamental to the continuity of our entire civilization. It ain't what you do, it's the way that you do it.

First, at the great risk of being immediately thrown into feminism jail, we need to be honest about the outrageous double standard. The likelihood of a young man being chastened for 'creepiness' is often directly proportionate to his sex appeal. And a lot of the more trivial stuff is just humiliation for the sake of viral clout on social media. There's a trend of young women showing up at gyms in lingerie or skintight pyjamas and then posting shaming videos of the men who – shock horror – look at them.

Second, women actually do want men to chat them up. Countless surveys show that women still expect men to make the first move because the things they often find most attractive are confidence, humour and the ability to deliver prosperity. A self-assured and respectful proposition is often a firm indicator of all three. But many men are now scared of making a move because they're afraid of being smeared as a mini-Weinstein and afraid of rejection.

The answer is to have some manners, take no for an answer and retain the confidence to try again with some-body else. Instead many young men are giving up altogether and spending far too much time in the company of Pornhub. A man's innate desire to find and keep a partner is not something to be ashamed of. It's often chan-nelled into getting and staying fit, competing for status and wealth, and summoning the courage to develop fast-vanishing social skills like talking to strangers and shining in a group. These are all objectively good things.

For all of the attempts to feminise men by demeaning masculinity and celebrating the fawning or blubbering types, there is no evidence that women actually want it.

Other recent studies show that women are now more prone to *saying* they want a gentle man who's in touch with his emotions, but when it actually happens in practice they make a hasty retreat. That's the logical consequence of pushing a societal ideal that sounds good on paper but is fundamentally at odds with everything we understand by instinct.

Being a man involves having the confidence to take chances and risk humiliation. We should celebrate that and teach young men how to do it with manners and in a way that doesn't make anybody feel uncomfortable. It's not that complicated. We've been doing it for 300,000 years.

I'm surrounded by plenty of strong women and always have been. They're not shy about telling me what they think. I am yet to meet a woman who honestly prefers any of the sanitised alternatives to a confident man who's full of competitive energy, loyalty, vitality, self-control and the insatiably burning desire to protect and to win. Whisper it, but they also quite like it when we pick up the bill, hold open the door or lug bags of compost in from the car. These are basic, instinctive and protective principles of decency.

We have manufactured the disastrous current crisis of masculinity on behalf of the other half of the population without ever checking if they wanted it in the first place. What could be more misogynistic than that? We'll emerge from the crisis by simply encouraging men to do the one thing they can do better than anything without even having to try. Be a man!

8. BE A WOMAN!

Unsurprisingly I am less of an authority on femininity, but I can see that the same cultural levers have been pulled to dilute it. Typically feminine traits – nurturing, emotional intelligence, cooperation, the desire and skill to create harmony – have been reframed as weaknesses in a culture of aggressive careerism.

There's a longstanding myth that women need to behave more like men to get ahead in the workplace. In my experience, the opposite is true. A team of excitable men needs nothing more than a dose of female orderliness and calm.

The laudable drive for women's equality has been remarkably successful at breathtaking speed but has negative consequences too. We've encouraged the idea that women who want to prioritise their families over their careers are somehow traitors to their gender. That finding fulfilment in motherhood is somehow less valuable to society than scaling corporate ladders.

NFL star Harrison Butker, a devout Catholic, was roundly lambasted over a commencement address he gave to graduating students at a private Catholic college in 2024. His offence was to suggest that female students in the audience should be as excited about their future families as their future promotions.

'I can tell you that my beautiful wife Isabelle would be the first to say that her life truly started when she began living her vocation as a wife and as a mother,' he said, choking up with tears. 'I'm on this stage today, and able to be the man I am, because I have a wife who leans into her vocation.'

The subsequent backlash predictably equated his message with calling for all women to be chained to the kitchen stove. Hundreds of thousands signed a petition for him to be fired by his team. Forgotten in the furore was that his audience of Catholics, at a Catholic school, burst into an adoring ovation.

Surely the point of equality is to give women equal choice and opportunities, not a command? Some women choose to prioritise their personal attainment. Some still choose to prioritise homemaking. Both things are fulfilling and valuable.

From my vantage point the 'have it all' myth has heaped undue pressures and burdens on women because it actually means 'do it all'. The rush to prove that women can do anything men can do has generally resulted in them having to do the things men can't do as well.

There certainly are kickass female leaders who work an 80-hour week while raising four children in a spotless household and mastering yoga. It's a feat usually made possible by a team of nannies, housekeepers, personal trainers and chefs. For everyone else there is stress, burnout and anxiety. And neither sex is benefiting here. Nobody is happy. Women in their 40s are increasingly dependent on antidepressants – including one in five women in the US.

My personal favourite of the crimes against feminism is being beautiful – or trying to. The theory being that our concept of beauty was crafted by men and the only possible incentive to look good is pleasing men. Total nonsense.

Many women feel good when they look good and that's a perfectly good reason for doing it. Amping up the allure breeds confidence, swagger and energy. How outrageously sexist to suggest they're only doing it for male benefit!

As for the stereotypical 'social construct' of beauty, I'd bet my house that if you travelled back in time and asked 100 cavemen whether they'd rather hang out with Rosie O'Donnell or Scarlett Johansson, you'd get the same 100 answers. Shave your head and grow your armpit hair if you want to – that's entirely your business – but don't chastise women who want to look good.

Women have many distinct natural qualities, just as men do. The ability to read emotional undercurrents, to build consensus and to nurture are not consolation prizes. Until the gender wars began, it was innately understood that all of humanity is based on the complementary inter-play of our *combined* forces. Now, do you need me to open that jar?

9. BE GRATEFUL NOT HATEFUL

'Live every day as if it's your last because one day you'll be right.'

If I have anything that can be described as a philosophy of life, it would really be as simple as that. I've seen these words attributed to everybody from Steve Jobs to Muhammad Ali and Ray Charles. Personally I first heard them many years ago from Matthew Harding, a highly successful insurance broker and vice-chairman of Chelsea

Football Club, who tragically died in a terrible helicopter crash aged just 42.

The provenance isn't as important as the prescience. It reminds me to absolutely never take anything for granted. There's nothing more sobering, grounding and levelling than the inevitability of our own mortality. It eliminates a lot of the froth and nonsense. If you got out of bed tomorrow morning knowing it was your last day on earth, would you want to spend it brooding over your enemies and cursing your luck?

Or would you choose to be thankful for your faculties and rapaciously enthusiastic about enjoying the people and opportunities still in front of you? I'd be squarely in the latter camp, with a decent amount of time allotted for a valedictory Montecristo cigar and a big glass of Château Margaux.

I think being relentlessly grateful is the absolute antithesis of being woke. I see woke as a mindset of constant struggle and victimhood, even when it's well intentioned. All the world is a battle for justice between marginalised victims and their vindictive overlords. It's an endless quest to identify the reasons why other people are beating you down; why you're offended, why it's not fair. And it's so full of vengeful hatred. Hate your opponents, hate your country, hate your history, hate the rich, hate the police, hate men, hate fun, hate steak.

I'm acutely aware that woke does not have a monopoly on hateful scorn. There are plenty of extremist blowhards and full-on racists who don't seem very grateful for the world either. The difference is we tend to push them to the fringes of society, where they belong. Woke was an ascendant cultural phenomenon espoused universally as a solution to all the world's injustices.

Keyboard warriors often describe me as 'hateful' and accuse me of 'hate-mongering' because they are triggered by my playful antagonism and the belligerent defence of my own opinions. The truth is I use the word 'hate' extremely sparingly because I don't feel it. I find many people laughable, ludicrous, lamentable and loathsome, but I don't hate them. Hatred is blinding, uncompromising and a massive waste of energy.

Gratitude has the complete opposite effect and I have it in spades. I'm grateful for my health and the health of my family. I'm grateful for my friends and their company, especially having lived several times through the gut-punch of losing a friend far too early. I'm battle-hardened by covering horrific news stories but never so much that I'm not acutely grateful my own loved ones are not the people involved. I'm grateful that I have an exciting job and that I encounter many people who challenge and stimulate me, even when it's in the form of extreme annoyance.

It's impossible to be grateful and hateful at the same time. Honestly, try it yourself. Next time you get some good news on a phone call you were dreading, or realise your missing keys were always in your coat pocket, you'll notice that gratitude elbows everything else out of its way. It's the 800-pound gorilla of emotions, the roaring silverback of sentiments, and if you must be 'in touch with' any of them I highly recommend it's this one.

I regularly remind myself that I have a lot but am entitled to nothing. Anything can disappear in a puff of smoke. Think about how many people would give up everything material they have to spend one more day with someone they've lost or to have the physical capability to go for a walk in the fresh air and play football with their kids. Walking up a big flight of stairs is a real grind – until you can't do it any more.

A bit of gratitude goes a long way to unlocking all of the other things I've talked about and believe in. It's a reason to be optimistic. It's a powerful incentive to get off your backside and shed some sweat on getting things done. It might even make you a bit more pleasant to be around.

10. BACK YOURSELF

Most people put humongous effort into hiding this, but it's almost immediately visible and impossible to ignore. You can see it from the opposite end of a corridor, across a crowded nightclub and even in photographs. The temptation is to deny it's happening instead of facing up to it, which can lead to intense embarrassment. I'm not talking about male pattern baldness but about insecurity; a stubborn mind barnacle that can eventually be chiselled off with practice.

Besides bona fide psychopaths, everybody wrestles with self-doubt. The difference is that high achievers tend to barrel through it. They're sharp enough to realise their chips are down but their gut says they will find a way to win them back. Not everybody finds this easy, but it really comes down to a simple question: if you don't believe in yourself then why should anybody else?

Most of the great figures of history are bold, polarising and unconventional. When enough time has passed they are defined by their stunning achievements and not the mockery, abuse and failures they invariably endured by daring to be different. They're very often propelled by an unquenchable self-belief that seems belligerent and reckless until, eventually, everybody else believes it too.

Winston Churchill spent his 25th birthday as a prisoner of war in South Africa, just weeks after he'd arrived as a correspondent to cover the Boer War. Famously he escaped by scaling a wall, hiding in a coal mine and smuggling himself onto a freight train. He then fought in the war for six months before returning to Britain as a hero.

Years later as First Lord of the Admiralty, Churchill masterminded the disastrous Gallipoli campaign and resigned in disgrace. He gradually mounted an implausible political comeback, which collapsed yet again into a wilderness decade during which he faced financial ruin and his repeated warnings about the Nazi threat were ignored. Everybody knows what happened next.

Henry Ford revolutionised modern industry by developing the moving assembly line; fundamentally transforming manufacturing and making cars affordable for the masses, but before that he was derided for his outlandish conspiracy theories and ventures like the 'Peace Ship', an amateur diplomatic voyage to end World War I, which was essentially the original Greta Thunberg 'Freedom Flotilla'.

Elon Musk is one of the richest men in history and the unquestionable genius behind some of the most innovative and influential companies in the world. His early career was marked by repeated rejection and derision until he used his share of the PayPal spoils to personally fund Tesla and SpaceX through near-bankruptcy as investors deserted him.

SpaceX was about to hit the wall after three failed rocket launches but the fourth succeeded and Musk's business is now integral to all of modern space exploration. SpaceX's reusable rockets, returning from space to be plucked from the air by giant chopsticks, are the greatest leap forward since the development of rockets themselves.

To this day Elon is taunted, abused and written off by detractors who lament his maverick personal life, his brash political interventions and his forthright predictions on AI supremacy, the end of humanity and colonising Mars. There is no doubt he suffers for this and palpably craves popularity, but he keeps on doggedly driving onwards and he always bets on himself. How could anyone bet against him?

There is no success without failure and no failure without risk. Nothing spectacular ever happens in a comfort zone. There are many valid, logical reasons for being risk-averse and I begrudge nobody who achieves consummate and comfortable mediocrity. Personally, I like daredevil adventurousness and audacity. On paper my whole adult life has been triumph and failure, boom and bust, but I learn a lot from the bust and I back myself to win the next round.

Confidence is contagious. If you can articulate a clear vision of what you want and why you want it, you'll be amazed at how readily other people will get behind you. You're making their lives easier by giving them a tangible aim and you're uniting them behind a shared purpose. The worst leaders are the flip-floppers who struggle to say what they want because they haven't figured it out for themselves.

You don't need to do a management course or start visiting a guru to back yourself. It's nothing more sophisticated than having confidence in your own abilities and confidence in your work rate and fortitude when they fall short. Society is now saturated with people who find all manner of reasons to forecast failure, for themselves and other people. Instead of fantasising about what could go wrong, try asking yourself what could go right.

11. DON'T BE A HYPOCRITE

Hypocrisy and wokery are like hand and glove. Being a hypocrite is not just a familiar trait among wokies but essential to their existence. It's the rank double standard that justifies preaching about carbon emissions while flying in a private jet, preaching about kindness while savaging detractors and preaching about the evils of milk while wearing leather shoes.

Woke postures as anti-racist and anti-sexist but supports the state-sponsored discrimination of heterosexual men and white people as a means of achieving social justice. It protests for the rights of the downtrodden at marches filmed on smartphones made in Chinese sweat-shops. It assembles at Glastonbury Festival under the banner of world peace while chanting 'death to the IDF' in a field that will be left blanketed by 2,000 tonnes of garbage and disposable tents. It wears the Palestinian keffiyeh while chiding Jamie Oliver's 'jerk rice' as cultural appropriation.

It's a mindset that sets an impossible standard of purity for everybody other than the people who are tarring and feathering those who fail to meet it. By this preposterous standard, lifelong feminists became bigoted transphobes, colour-blind idealists became racists, the most modern and tolerant countries in the modern world became pariahs. And what were the wokest among us doing during this period of sanctimony and shaming? Usually the exact opposite of everything they told you to do.

Ellen DeGeneres built a TV empire on the promotion of kindness and tolerance. She signed off every show by saying 'be kind to one another' and hawked a 'Be Kind' subscription box, which spawned benevolent spinoff products like a $48 skin-firming serum under the label of 'Kind Science'. The show collapsed and DeGeneres effectively retired when multiple former and current employees accused her of fostering a 'toxic' workplace marred by bullying, discrimination and sexual harassment.

Nothing repels fair-minded people as abruptly and fiercely as stinking hypocrisy. It awakens an inner sense of outrage and a common-sense barometer that screams 'Hey, wait a minute, you just told me you believed in *this*.' Of all the roles I play in the public arena, none are as universally popular as my job as the self-appointed sheriff of the hypocrisy police.

You don't have to be woke to be a hypocrite, but it helps. I revile hypocrisy wherever it presents itself, which is why I've challenged so many Trump supporters over why they're furiously opposed to US backing for Ukraine but perform somersaults to explain their support for their military backing of Israel. You can change your mind and evolve your positions as the facts change. Just don't be disingenuous and dishonest if you're basing your opinions only on tribalism, ideology or loyalty.

I think socialist whingebag Jeremy Corbyn would have made a disastrous prime minister as I disagree with so much of his worldview, but I do respect that he's been doggedly beating the same drum at the back of Parliament for 42 years. He's consistent and principled, even if his principles are consistently wrong. Boris Johnson on the other hand, who actually *was* a disastrous prime minister, changed his views for convenience or crowd-pleasing as often as I change socks.

The complete opposite of a hypocrite is someone who is authentic, sincere and principled. It commands respect. I'm sure I sometimes fall short on all three counts, but at least I've got the moral compass to recognise them as aspirational qualities. It gets to the core of trying to be a better person in a better society. You can't get it right all the time, but you can be honest about your shortcomings and true to your values. Alternatively you can just 'be kind'.

12. PUT THE PHONE DOWN

Technology seemed to be booming in the late 1980s, around the time I landed my first job on the *Sun*. Big TVs, VHS players, handheld video cameras, the Walkman, dictaphones, boomboxes, gaming consoles, digital calculators, home computers. You could easily spend a year's salary on this revolutionary new tech and it could easily fill your garage. Every single one of those things is now accessible from our pockets.

Factor in the endless time-sucking vortex of the internet and social media and it's really not remotely surprising that we're all hooked on phones. I say 'we' deliberately because this one is a work in progress rather than a record of achievement. Sometimes I put my phone in my pocket after browsing X and then immediately pull it back out to check again before I even realise what I'm doing.

There's a growing trend for idyllic off-grid retreats and 'digital detoxes' involving wilderness log cabins and kale. I would rather garotte myself with rusty swords while eating a glass sandwich than pay for that. But I'm rapidly coming around to the idea that everyone needs regular self-imposed smartphone breaks and a spoonful of real life.

Social media was the baking powder behind the rapid rise of woke and retains the key ingredients for propelling a new wave of silliness. It's tribal, global and powered by outrage, which make a perfect breeding ground for bad ideas and purity purges. It's not going anywhere, and frankly I wouldn't want it to, but as it gets ever more popular we have to learn to steel ourselves with a tough outer armour of common sense.

The inflammatory do-or-die arguments we have online are worlds away from how we conduct ourselves in the real world. Scandals that erupt on our timelines remain a complete mystery to people who abstain altogether. The most imperative conflicts and debates on X have no impact whatsoever on tangible things that really matter like our personal relationships, our physical health and whether we can pay the bills. I love the vibrant riot of competing opinions, ideas and solutions, but I recognise that there's a more important world over the brow of my screen.

I worry that young people simply don't get that. A whole generation of kids now doesn't know anything other than a culture that depends on smartphones and the internet. They're exposed to a relentless and limitless supply of content and language that no parent would ever show to them and to judgement and standards that dangerously warp their expectations of reality.

The most obvious problem is their expectation of instant gratification and shortcuts. Everything should be available instantly and effortlessly. The most disturbing problem is the substitution of human relationships with synthetic versions that resemble reality but are anything but. The unstoppable rise of AI is making this exponentially worse.

Personal relationships – whether romantic, platonic, familial or professional – take a lot of hard work. There's embarrassment, disappointment, anger, frustration, impatience and resentment. They are a tangled web of competing interests, expectations and compromises. AI can already plausibly deputise as a friend, counsellor or mentor and do it without any of the baggage. But it is only a product whose existence depends on monetising your screen time and absorbing your data to perpetuate itself.

A lot of people can no longer find their way to the local train station without following a GPS map on their phones and find themselves in a world of pain when they have no WiFi. It took just one generation for physical maps to become antiques used by hobbyists and the elderly.

At the current rate of development, kids won't be able to compose their own sentences without being connected to the internet. They won't create new or groundbreaking art or music because of the synthetic, effortless alternatives generated by copying centuries of human labour and ingenuity that came before them. They will have no incentive or ability to build the social skills needed for the travails of real-world relationships if we give them unfettered access to synthetic companionship that pretends to be the real thing.

Just look at the explosion of pornography and the disturbing rise in porn addiction. Swathes of young people are hooked on immediate, unlimited satisfaction from unrealistic and sometimes disturbing portrayals of sex. It leaves them with distorted expectations for the real world and it robs them of the desire to go out and work for something that's supposed to be a challenging exercise in social skills, self-improvement and managing human complexity.

Many European countries, including France, Belgium, the Netherlands and Italy, have now introduced full or partial bans on smartphones in schools. Australia is in the process of banning access to social media for children aged below 16. It remains to be seen how easily it can be enforced, but I think this should be universal. As a parent you don't want to deprive your child of anything other people are experiencing, but that instinct is bulldozed by the duty to protect them from harm that is now indisputable.

We all trade certain liberties for conveniences when it comes to using anything online. My phone listens to my conversations, knows where I am, what I have planned and who I'm with. All of the apps I use are training themselves on my private data and some of it is used to sell me products. I put up with that because they make my life easier. We all do.

However, I want to live in a civil world of joyous, complicated personal relationships in which people develop the skills and knowledge to think for themselves, make things for themselves and innovate for themselves. It's literally the essence of humanity.

Smartphones have revolutionised our lives in endless positive ways and AI is capable of doing the same on a far greater scale. It might well cure cancer or crack the code for a perfect system of government that ends starvation and conflict. But what's the point in solving all of humanity's problems if it's at the cost of everything it means to be human?

13. WEEDS ALWAYS COME BACK

Woke is dead but thankfully this does not mean that all of the woke people are dead or that all of their ideas have disappeared for eternity. They're still walking among us, zombie-like, and clinging to the entrails of the censorious system they thought would conquer the world. The key difference is that excessive wokery is now met with pillorying rather than pandering.

The silenced majority is back in charge. What felt like an ascendant and dominant social force has very quickly turned into the subject of eye-rolling weariness and the preserve of a radical minority. Hilariously and aptly there was a modest attempt to cancel the live audience launch event for this book over fears of picketing protestors. Five years ago it would have been axed in a storm of headlines. Instead it was resolved in a brief phone call with the venue's owner, who apparently found the irony as amusing as I did.

This triumph of common sense was never about extinguishing the ideas but the methods. I don't agree that men are the devil incarnate or that meat is murder. I don't long for the destruction of the imperialist West or de-funding the police. I don't agree that biological men should compete against women or that anyone is really benefiting from gay pride rainbows on cans of beer.

The difference is that I'm more than happy to debate those ideas with anybody. I'll read or listen to thoughtful counterpoints that challenge my own certainty. I do this every day on my show and in my spare time too. In the highly unlikely event that I change my mind about any of these things, I'll gladly admit it and explain why.

Wokeness became a crisis because of its absolutism. It was a moral crusade for justice, meaning its advocates would settle for nothing less than total victory. It was of such singular importance to them that all means were justified, including the defenestration and silencing of critics. It meant the denial of facts, reason, science and logic whenever they were inconvenient. There are few things more disturbing than any form of authority that tells you that objective reality is not reality just to get what it wants.

These are illiberal, anti-democratic tactics, which stifled debate and scared people into compliance. They made everybody more miserable. The tinderbox of the pandemic and social media caused the explosion, but the methods are tried and tested. They've been preferred weapons in the authoritarian's armoury for a very long time. And that's why I have no doubt we'll see them again.

Bad habits and bad ideas have a knack for returning. It's as true in society as it is in daily life. You can quit smoking cigarettes or lay off the biscuits, but unless you deal with the root cause, whether it's an outlet for stress or a lack of stimulation, you'll be back in the cookie jar before you even realise.

That's why communism hangs around like a bad smell. After any cycle of economic turmoil there is normally a startling surge in the number of young people who suddenly think Marxism sounds great. The repeated failures of a totalitarian system that cultivates stagnant, bloated enterprises and empty shelves are quickly forgotten in the temptation for simple answers to complicated problems.

To be fair to the young idealists, the root cause of today's youth dissatisfaction in that case is income inequality. Too many young people can't afford a house, can't afford to have children and can't afford to plan for the future. The average age of a first-time homeowner is 35 in London. In New York it's now 37, which might partially explain the popularity of avowed socialist Zohran Mamdani.

Nobody wants to dismantle or overthrow a system that's working perfectly well for them and this one isn't working for everyone. I understand that. I just have no desire to break it all apart and replace it with something that's demonstrably even worse. Like most sensible people, I'm an extreme realist who believes all good solutions are based on compromise and clear thinking in the face of incompetent lunacy.

If the definition of madness is repeating the same mistakes and expecting different results, the antidote has to be common sense. That little internal voice that reliably calls bullshit and faithfully tells us that if it seems too good to be true, it usually is. No doubt you'll be needing it again in future.

For the time being, relax. Kick your shoes off. Feel the weight lifting from your shoulders and breathe in the freedom to say what you please, ignore the histrionics and follow your gut instinct. It's been a rough few years of demoralising conflict and spiteful sanctimony, but the energy is with us now. The momentum is all ours. There's a liberating sense of a crisis averted and an unexpected opportunity to do something better.

So yes, bad ideas and bad habits always come back. They're like ugly garden weeds. The difference is that next time we'll be ready for them. More people than ever are standing by with their trowels, ready to yank them up from the roots. Common sense is a potent weedkiller and it's our most understated superpower. Simple, unfashionable and completely unstoppable when enough people use it.

ACKNOWLEDGEMENTS

There are many brilliant people who have helped me with this book.

Most notably, Alex Campbell, the multi-talented Executive Editor of *Piers Morgan Uncensored* who runs my show and has also written every monologue since we launched three years ago. He's done a lot of the heavy lifting on material for *Woke Is Dead*, and I am hugely appreciative. Thanks, Alex!

I'd also like to thank my editor, Oliver Malcolm, for steering the ship so masterfully through the whole process from first to final draft. All writers need a smart, ballsy editor who can also save them from themselves, and they don't come smarter or ballsier than Oli.

A small army at my publishers, HarperCollins, has been incredibly supportive: in the UK, I'd like to thank Charlie Redmayne, Sarah Emsley, Huw Armstrong, Simon Gerratt, Orlando Mowbray and Isabel Prodger. In the US, Brian Murray, Jean Marie Kelly, Kamrun Nesa and Sophia Wilhelm. And everyone in the sales teams on both sides of the pond.

I'd also like to thank Tom Whiting for his astute copy-editing, and Mark Bolland for his expert fact-checking.

Heartfelt gratitude goes to my magnificent literary agent Eugenie Furniss at 42, and to my fabulous executive assistant and Anchor Producer, Kerrie Hutton, and equally fabulous former PA, Tracey Chapman, who retired this year after 20 years at the Morgan coalface.

And to my wife Celia, my parents Gabrielle and Glynne, and my children Spencer, Stanley, Bertie and Elise, for collectively keeping my feet firmly grounded in reality!